WINNING
In Small Claims
COURT

*A Step-by-Step Guide for Trying
Your Own Small Claims Cases*

WINNING
In Small Claims
COURT

A Step-by-Step Guide for Trying Your Own Small Claims Cases

By
Judge William E. Brewer

CAREER PRESS
3 Tice Road, P.O. Box 687
Franklin Lakes, NJ 07417
1-800-CAREER-1
201-848-0310 (NJ and outside U.S.)
Fax: 201-848-1727

WINNING IN SMALL CLAIMS COURT
Cover design by Rob Johnson Design
Printed in the U.S.A. by Book-mart Press

To order this title, please call toll-free 1-800-CAREER-1 (NJ and Canada: 201-848-0310) to order using VISA or MasterCard, or for further information on books from Career Press.

Library of Congress Cataloging-in-Publication Data

Brewer, William E.
    Winning in small claims court : a step-by-step guide for trying
your own small claims cases / by William E. Brewer.
      p.   cm.
    Includes index.
    ISBN 1-56414-374-0
    1. Small claims courts--United States--Popular works.   I. Title.
KF8769.Z9B738   1998
347.73'28DC21   98-30415

Acknowledgments

This work would not have been possible without help and inspiration from many, including Dusty Rainbolt, who first said yes to my writing; Roger Kessinger, a publisher; Nancy Ballance, editor extraordinaire; Mills Fitzner, a man with a kind word at the right time; Dick Fagan and John Hoey, my teachers; Greg Ellstrom, my friend and a writer; and to those citizens with gumption and a gripe who know that they will still find justice in the courts of this great country.

CONTENTS

Introduction   11

PART I
FIRST THINGS FIRST

Chapter 1: What Goes On Here?   17

Chapter 2: How I Know   21

Chapter 3: Are These Courts Really Small?   25

Chapter 4: The Briefest of Boring Details   27

PART II
JUST THE FACTS AND JUST THE LAW

Chapter 5: The Cause of Action   33

Chapter 6: What Kind of Claim Do You Have?   39

Chapter 7: Torts: The Hurts We Suffer   43

Chapter 8: Contracts: The Promises We Make   47

Chapter 9: Contract Cases: Promises Others Have Made   57

Chapter 10: Is the Case Contract, Tort, or Both?   67

Chapter 11: High Crimes, Misdemeanors, and Ordinances   71

PART III
LET THE WAR GAME BEGIN

Chapter 12: Getting Free (or Nearly Free) Good Legal Advice   75

Chapter 13: Settlement: Winning Without Fighting   79

Chapter 14: Negotiating Your Settlement   87

Chapter 15: When Should You Hire a Lawyer?   91

Chapter 16: Going For It: Your First Trip to the Courthouse   95

Chapter 17: Filing Your Small Claims Suit   97

Chapter 18: A Tour of the Courthouse   105

PART IV
TRIAL NOTEBOOK

Chapter 19: Primer: Anatomy of a Trial   109

Chapter 20: Final Trial Preparation   111

Chapter 21: Your Trial Notebook   127

PART V
NICE WORK, NICE JUDGMENT. WHAT NOW?

Chapter 22: Collecting Your Judgment 137

Chapter 23: The End 143

Chapter 24: Forms 145

    A. Complaint/Statement of Claim 147
    B. Summons 148
    C. Answer and Counterclaim 149
    D. Third Party Complaint/Statement of Claim 150
    E. Consent Order 152
    F. Dismissal After Consent Order 153
    G. Affidavit for Entry of Default Judgment 154
    H. Consent Judgment 155
    I. Consent Judgment/Payment Agreement 156
    J. Judgment Payment Agreement 157
    K. Affidavit and Notice of Default 158

PART VI
APPENDICES

Appendix 1: Questions to Ask the Clerk 161

Appendix 2: More Definitions 163

Appendix 3: State Courts and Quirks 169

Index 181

"No person shall be deprived of life, liberty or property without due process of the law and no state shall deny any person within its jurisdiction equal protection of the laws."
—U.S. Constitution

Introduction

Do you want to sue somebody? Has someone decided they have a claim against you? Have you received a nasty lawyer letter demanding payment of an unjust claim or amount? Are you a businessperson who for years has seen your profits chipped away by small debts and accounts owed to you, but that would be too expensive to collect through a collection agency or attorney? Have you ever seen yourself as a lawyer? Have you fantasized about standing before a judge pointing out that the witness, whom you have just grilled into submission, is the guilty party?

You've probably been in a situation similar to those just mentioned, and found yourself at a loss as to what to do. The choices seem to fall into three categories: 1) Go through the time and expense of hiring a lawyer; 2) Do nothing and give up whatever legal claims you may have against others; 3) If the claim is against you, pay it because it is just too complicated to try and have it dismissed. But wait! How about going to court on your own? Usually, this option is not even considered, because it is too intimidating. But you *can* be successful in litigating your own case, and if the idea sounds appealing, then you will enjoy *Winning in Small Claims Court.*

My interest in writing this manual was prompted, in large part, by seeing citizens come into my court with viable claims and losing simply because they didn't have any idea about how to put together their case. This not only makes bad law, but also undermines public faith in a civil justice system already subject to stinging and far-ranging criticism.

People often have the impression that lawyers possess a mysterious magic key to solving legal entanglements. I admit that at one time I felt this way, too. But when I walked into a courtroom for the first time as a new law graduate, shaking, and not sure what traps had been laid for me there, I began to come to the realization that solving legal mysteries is not magical at all—it is simply knowledge of and familiarity with the territory. This book is a simple yet comprehensive map of that legal territory, accompanied by plenty of interesting stories and humor to help present the legal issues in easy-to-understand terms.

Courts Are People, Not Buildings

The American legal system is made up of people; it is not just austere-looking buildings, where obscure legal theories thrive and become more and more unfathomable to the citizens governed by them. My children's friends are often shocked when they first learn that I am a judge after they have mostly seen me in blue jeans, running shoes, and a T-shirt. Somehow, it's hard to picture a judge as a regular person, too. But our legal system is made up of a lot of ordinary people striving to create and uphold a system of justice that is true to the goals and ideals of the Constitution.

Small claims courts give new and effective access to a legal form where legal disputes that naturally arise every day in an increasingly urban society can be resolved quickly, cheaply, and judiciously. These courts have been created and are being expanded just for you. They are the real "people's courts." The rules are simplified here so that just about any-one can have a claim heard, whether the person is suing or being sued, without the assis-tance (or interference) of an attorney.

Lawyers don't usually practice in small claims court. The amounts in dispute are gen-erally small, which means they can't make a buck, so they avoid small claims courts like cats avoid a garden hose.

What This Book Will Do For You

Winning in Small Claims Court is not an exhaustive study of the intricacies of the law. It is an approach to preparing a case for a level of courts that emphasize informality. Most of these courts are not bogged down by technical rules of procedure or evidence. These courts exist solely for the citizen, and the approach of this book is to help the citizen be ready for the courts.

Presenting a case to a judge is simply telling a story. It is the same as telling a story to anyone: Say it completely, but say it plainly. You can do this by deciding what facts are im-portant and telling them to the judge in a way he or she will understand. This book will help you be comprehensive and clear.

Winning in Small Claims Court is for people who want to sue or defend a lawsuit over a small to moderate sum of money without a lawyer, and win. An attorney's job is to gain the best legal outcome for a client based on the facts of the client's case and the law. This book is designed to teach the average citizen to accomplish that without the unnecessary expense of a lawyer's fees. It is designed so that with a few hours of preparation, you can try your case before a small claims judge as well as or better than an attorney would (you are naturally much more interested in it, anyway). Legally trying a case is a civilized (usually) substitute for war. Being better armed with the legal knowledge you need greatly improves your odds of winning.

Winning in Small Claims Court contains principles, methods, and concrete examples based upon years of experience in small claims court. It starts out by helping you determine whether you have a case at all, and the initial steps to take if you decide that you do. The book then explains the law as it relates to the typical cases that appear in small claims courts. It gives you a tour of the courthouse and explains its inner workings and explains all the steps of the lawsuit, from filing to collecting the judgment. If you are a defendant, you will learn all the available defenses and how to put them to work for you. Whether you are the plaintiff or the defendant, the book will familiarize you with the strategies of the opposition in this civilized battle.

The book also provides you with a portable tool to take to court with you to guide you through your trial experience: a trial notebook (see Part IV). You can keep it open in front of you in court and refer to it during the trial. It will enable you to stand up in court and say, "Your honor, I object," and explain why.

The point of view in this book is from the side of the plaintiff (or the potential plaintiff, if a lawsuit has not actually been filed yet). But all the principles involved apply whether you are the plaintiff or the defendant. Each discussion includes notes to defendants explaining how a point relates to those in the position of *defending* a legal claim.

You may even be reading this book because you are already involved in a legal conflict. The principles in this book will help you handle this conflict, and will help you prevent legal entanglements in the future. There are many simple, common sense things you can do in your everyday personal and professional life to avoid conflict.

This book is for everyone; it's like having a lawyer in your pocket, but less cumbersome and noisy—and it won't charge you by the hour. It is about winning, which in the law means gaining the best legal outcome from your dispute. This is what lawyers get paid to do, but when you pursue your own legal cause, you may feel the wild exhilaration of victory from crushing your opposition in a hard-fought trial. However, getting your best result does not mean emotional fireworks, only the full satisfaction of having made the absolute best of your circumstances.

Ben Franklin said, "If you want a servant who will serve you well, and one you will like, serve yourself." This book will help you serve yourself well and will increase your chance of success.

First Things First

Chapter 1

What Goes on Here?

Sometimes the reasons that bring people to small claims court are not what you might expect. And sometimes they are. Let's take a look at a few disputes that found their way to a small claims court.

Don Rudd and Joe Wilson had been next-door neighbors for five years. They didn't get along from the start, with their relationship progressively going downhill. They were involved in an escalating scheme to get under each other's skin in the name of protecting their God-given rights.

The first year, Rudd built a fence and Wilson's dog dug tunnels under it. Rudd was forced to shore up the gaps in his barricade with cement blocks and discarded telephone poles. Very unsightly!

Rudd, for his part, could never find quite the right place for his grass clippings, so he put them in the far rear corner of his yard—the corner shared by Wilson. The pile of clippings grew higher and wider, eventually spreading well over the property line. This made Wilson extremely angry, especially after he had asked Rudd several times, as nicely as he could, to clean up the mess. Rudd never got around to it.

Tuesday was garbage day in Rudd and Wilson's neighborhood. The sanitation pick-up was made between 6:30 and 7:30 in the morning. When Wilson's work schedule changed, and he began to go to work after the morning rush hour, he put his trash at the curb the night before to make sure he didn't miss the pick-up. Sometimes, he had more garbage than the cans would hold, and inevitably the loose garbage would end up strewn all over the front of Rudd's yard. Rudd would become livid every time this happened.

Rudd decided to get even, once and for all. With his wife's help, he set upon a plan. One hot Friday night in the summer, under the cover of darkness, he emptied a large lawn bag of grass clippings onto Wilson's central air conditioning unit.

On Saturday morning, Rudd was casually raking his side yard with a steel tine garden rake when Wilson, with a very determined look and stride, walked across the yard toward him. "You covered my air conditioner with grass clippings," Wilson said, his voice strained.

Rudd kept raking.

"I'll give you 30 seconds to get over there and clean up that mess, or I'll..."

"Or what?" Rudd looked up, but kept the rake moving.

Wilson grabbed the rake in the middle with both hands as if to stop it. He was surprised by the strong grip Rudd had on it. The two men struggled only a second, then Rudd yanked the rake free and swung it once, hitting his neighbor in the back of the head with the steel edge of the business end.

Conveniently, Mrs. Rudd caught it all on 35mm film.

Later, they all came to court.

In another case, Jack Ratigan hired Plymouth Paint Company to caulk, seal, and restain the brown cedar front outside his barbecue-style restaurant. Ratigan's color choice was "Powerful Pink."

Plymouth painters did the job, and collected the $3,300 agreed-upon price.

Two weeks later, Ratigan began to notice brown splotches bleeding through the pink. By the third week, the restaurant looked like a giraffe with a fever.

Ratigan called Plymouth. Nick, the owner, said, "Sorry, no warranty," and hung up.

One day you may find yourself trying to resolve a dispute but having little success on your own. So, what do you do? Can you sue? Maybe. If you can, should you? If you should, can you win? Yes, you can.

Or you may be on the other side of the problem, the one being sued. Do you panic? A brief panic is acceptable, but it is better to plan instead.

The story of Rudd and Wilson and the case of the painting contract gone bad are just two examples of transactions gone awry that occur every day, and have occurred since people have lived near each other and have conducted commerce at any level. If people cannot resolve the disputes that come from these situations, they may end up in small claims court.

Like these disputes, the rules of law that will resolve them are ageless. They have existed pretty much in the same form since humans were forced to adjust their animal instincts to exist in society with other humans. Since then, people have been short-changed in the marketplace and have not gotten the benefit of their bargains, and they have been injured or had their property damaged by the intentional or negligent acts of others. As a result, the rules are pretty much as they always have been concerning these cases. And strangely, these rules make good common sense.

Like all courts, the serious business of small claims courts is to adjust the rights and obligations of the parties to meet the dictates of those rules society has laid down for conduct under the particular circumstances of each case.

These courts are different from others handling larger or different claims, because they allow you to participate in the legal fray without a lawyer. Before these courts were created, redress for these claims was not available to anyone who could not afford the high price of an attorney. Civil justice in any form was simply not available to a large segment of the population.

The legislatures that have created these courts have built a legal playing field for the ordinary citizen. In the process, they have put fun back into the challenge of living in a society plagued with risks of loss of money, property, and even personal integrity. What follows will arm you with the weapons, rules, and strategies you need to lodge a winning offense or defense when you show up for the game.

Chapter 2

How I Know

For the last 10 years, I have been a judge in a small claims court. During this time, I have enjoyed a parade of people with all sorts of legal problems. Most of the citizens who bring these cases before me and other judges in these courts have one trait in common: an independent streak that has compelled them to be their own lawyers on trial day. To many, it is a minor fantasy realized.

Over the last 30 years, television shows such as *Perry Mason* and *Law and Order* have fascinated and entertained us. There is always at least one law-related novel on the current best-seller list. We are a little mystified about the inner workings of the law, which attorneys have successfully kept secret from us. Over and over again, we get caught up in the drama of the courtroom, where words substitute for war machines. Real courtroom action, like the fictional kind, is full of suspense. We are never certain what the final outcome will be until we hear it from the judge's mouth.

Many of us have a secret desire to be in the shoes of the popular trial lawyer on the screen or in the news. We want to have a witness cringe under our pointed and searing cross-examination. Just once, we want to hear ourselves stand up and say with authority, "Your honor, I object!"

In practically every county and city in the country, small claims courts give us the opportunity to live this fantasy, and provide a cheap, efficient, and practical way solve legal disputes. Over the past few years, the legislatures that created these courts have expanded the types of cases they handle and increased the dollar amounts involved in those cases. Small claims courts were created to be a forum for the common citizen, free of technicalities and mystery, accessible to all. And now, the means of achieving success in these courts are available to everyone. So read on!

The great majority of small claims cases arise from everyday transactions, the same types of transactions that people have undertaken for thousands of years. You trade goods for goods, money for goods, services for services, or money for services as people have always done. Because these exchanges are so common, the rules of law that govern them have been uniform for a long time in every region of the country.

With a little preparation, and a well-thought-out approach, you can try your case in your local court better than most attorneys who might appear there.

Most attorneys who have appeared in my court have not been as well prepared as they should be. It is fair to say, however, that the parties represented by lawyers have done slightly better at judgment time than people who have represented themselves. I emphasize the word *slightly*. The lawyers hold a slight advantage only because they know how to prepare a case for trial a little better (if they in fact do prepare). Preparation is the key. I know that the win/loss ratio would improve for citizens if they simply knew how to put a case together and present it to the judge.

Lawyers and law firms are in business and the purpose of business is to make money. An attorney who charges more than $75 an hour (and almost all do) cannot make a profit if he or she spends time adequately preparing for and trying a case where the client is seeking a $500 recovery. If they agree to take such cases, these simple laws of economics control the degree to which they prepare. As a result, the attorney who shows up for a small claims case is usually one of three types: the "Pettifogger," the "Friend," or the "Novice."

The *Pettifogger* is the cheapest lawyer in town. His whole practice is contained in the appointment calendar he carries with him wherever he goes. It's stuffed with sticky yellow notes of calls not returned, appointments not met and court appearances missed. He advertises heavily and takes all cases for the lowest fee. The client sure gets what he or she pays for. Once the fee is collected, this lawyer figures that his only job is to show up. He does no work on the case beforehand and next to the same during trial.

A year ago, I was the attorney for a client in a small claims case in another county. The judge was scheduled to appear to begin trying cases at 1 p.m. At 12:58 p.m., a flustered, disheveled lawyer came into the courtroom and asked the bailiff to call for someone out in the hallway. The bailiff did and in walked the man's client. The lawyer introduced himself. They had obviously never met or even talked before. The lawyer asked the client to tell him her side of the case. She did so as the lawyer shuffled through papers and the client's file rested open on the attorney's briefcase.

The mystery of his case preparation played out before me and everyone else in the courtroom. After five minutes of listening to this citizen explain his whole case to his attorney (and to all of us in the courtroom), another lawyer got up and introduced himself to the Pettifogger. It was the attorney for the other side, who had just heard all of the Pettifogger's case! One attorney's fee in this case was not money well spent.

Fortunately, most state bar associations have been doing an increasingly good job of weeding out these parasites, but a few are still around. If you are opposing one in court, your joy in defeating him or her will be doubled by the appreciation of legitimate attorneys everywhere.

The *Friend* is a legitimate lawyer in his own law specialty. It might be Social Security law, worker's compensation, real estate, taxes, or government contracts. This attorney has taken the case because the client is a member of her church or the friend of another, more important client. She can't afford to investigate, do research, or organize her case in any meaningful way, so she "wings it."

With a little attention to your case, you can shoot down this kind of lawyer and watch the arc of his descent.

The *Novice* is the newest attorney in a large firm. The office has sent him to trial in the small claims court "to get experience." Here's a little-known secret: Law schools teach nothing about how to try a case. There is more practical information, *a whole lot more*, in this book than new lawyers paid $50,000 for in law school. They have never seen a trial, and may never have been in a courtroom before. They have probably done some research on the law, but may have no idea how it can be used. Therefore, there is nothing that makes the novice better qualified than you to represent yourself in court. All you need is average intelligence, enough curiosity to learn about preparing for and presenting your case at trial, and nerve to carry it through. You will be a winner.

CHAPTER 3

ARE THESE COURTS Really Small?

Not necessarily. Small claims are called this because there is a top dollar limit to the cases that can be heard there. Courts that are not small are not called big, but are known as courts of general or unlimited jurisdiction. The power of small claims courts is set by the legislatures that create each court. These courts are still considered small claims courts even though in some the top dollar limit is $25,000. If your claim has a value of greater than that, or greater than whatever the top dollar limit is in your local small claims court, you do not lose any rights. You just take your case to a different court.

Small claims courts were created and expanded for several reasons, not the least important being to take the pressure of increasing case loads off general jurisdiction ("big power") courts. The big power courts require big power lawyers who study and practice many years just to understand the convoluted technicalities that justify being paid big fees to handle these cases.

Small claims courts exist so that a regular citizen can prosecute or defend a claim without these technicalities, and especially without lawyers. In many, lawyers are prohibited.

The great majority of these courts have very simple rules. A *plaintiff* is the person who seeks to make a legal *complaint* against another person or entity, such as a business. The written claim that a plaintiff files in the court clerk's office to start a case is usually a concise statement of why the action is being brought and the amount being sued for. The *defendant* is the person who *defends* a claim being made against him or against his company. If the defendant files an answer or a countersuit, or a combination of both, his statement also takes the same simple form. The only legal requirement is that these statements be clear and complete enough so that the opposing sides understand one another's positions in the case.

In small claims cases, there is none of what lawyers know as *discovery*: formal requests to answer long and involved sets of questions, requests to produce documents and other information, or depositions requiring parties and witnesses to go to an attorney's office to answer questions about the case under oath before a court reporter (who, by the way, must also be paid). Discovery takes time.

In place of discovery, you may be required by your local rules to discuss your case fully with the other side in the courthouse before trial, or you may be required to submit your claim to a mediator or arbitrator, to have a kind of "mini-trial." (These forms of alternate resolution are discussed in Chapter 14.) In small claims courts, the rules of evidence, another source of mystery in the law, are usually relaxed. The main rule is that these exist to carry out justice, a goal often missed in courts muddled by arcane rules and procedures.

I used to take to court with me a small judge's gavel and set it on the bench before court began. The idea was to let everyone know that I believed that most of all, people wanted "a little justice" when they came to court. I still believe this to be true, and also believe that small claims court is the place you are most likely to find it.

Small claims courts exist to bring a little justice to those who bring their cases there. That they do it well, one case at a time, is restoring much lost faith in our judicial system.

CHAPTER 4

THE BRIEFEST OF BORING DETAILS

Before you leave on any journey, it is helpful to know the common road signs. In much the same way, courts have their own special road signs, or jargon.

Besides the signs that you will actually find there, such as where to find the restrooms or "Courtroom H," what follows is a summary of what law students learn in the first week of law school. Although definitions are painful, they are necessary. Getting them out of the way early is healthy. Therefore, I will present you with key terms you should know before you get involved in a small claims suit.

Jurisdiction, again, means power. When a court is created by a constitution or through legislative action, its power is defined and limited. Certain courts only have power to hear cases on certain subjects, such as traffic, family matters, or wills and estates. They can also be limited in dollar amount. If the amount sued for or claimed by either side in a lawsuit is more than the maximum set by law, the case cannot be heard there, because that court's power switch goes off.

Most small claims courts have the power to hear cases in the most common subject areas: contract disputes, accounts, and suits to recover to personal property damage, real estate, or injury to your body. They are said to have *broad* or *general* jurisdiction.

The powers of every court extend only to the border of a defined geographic area, too. This is why under your local rules, you may only be able to sue someone if he or she resides in your county or city. The power of your court, its jurisdiction, is limited to that area. This is true even for the U.S. Supreme Court, which has no power to hear cases involving disputes between other countries having no connection to the United States.

Courts exist to resolve disputes. A dispute does not exist unless someone has a gripe against someone else. If it is a type of gripe that a court will recognize as having legal merit, one that asks substantial questions about the rights of the parties, it is known as a *Legal Claim* or a *Cause of Action*. The *complainer* is the *plaintiff*. The court document that states the complaint is called, strangely, a *Complaint, Statement of Claim,* or *Petition for Relief*. You should know that the statements set out in the complaint are only *allegations* or *contentions*. This is what the plaintiff claims and hopes to prove is true. Allegations are not facts unless the plaintiff does prove them to a judge's satisfaction.

The person brought into court because someone has complained and who must defend his or her actions is the *defendant*. In response to a complaint, a defendant will file an *Answer*. If the defendant also has a claim against the plaintiff, he or she will countersue by filing a *counterclaim* that will be given or sent to the plaintiff. The people who are fighting it out in court are the called the *parties* (though it feels nothing like a party).

The actions brought in small claims courts fall into two broad categories: *contracts* and *torts*. A contract is an agreement between two or more people for the doing or not doing of a certain thing and is made up of the promises of each of the parties. Contracts can involve the exchange of all sorts of things: goods for money, services for money, goods for goods, or services for services. The plaintiff in a contract action comes to court complaining that the defendant has not lived up to his or her end of the deal. Defendants respond by claiming the many and various failings on the part of the plaintiff in the same contract. Considering the number and variety of these cases, sometimes it is amazing that commerce marches on at all.

A *tort* is a claimed violation of a private right other than the violation of a contract. Torts involve the rights not to have your person injured or your property damaged, either intentionally or through *negligence*. In a case of negligence the plaintiff claims that the defendant has broken the rule "You must be careful not to injure others." *Fraud* is a special kind of tort where the plaintiff claims he has been injured through trickery, misrepresentation, or deceit.

The defendant is brought into court by a process server giving him a copy of the complaint. In some small claims courts, this is done by certified mail. There is a *summons* attached to it, which tells the defendant how to respond, orally or in writing, and how much time he or she has to respond in order to prevent a judgment being entered against him or her without a trial, by *default*.

A *motion* is a written or oral request asking a judge to order something specific done. This will be the judge's *order*.

The complaint or statement of claim, answer, and counterclaim, and discovery documents—that is, all of the documents filed by the parties—are called the *pleadings*.

There are two kinds of law that govern a court case. The first are the rules of *procedural law*. These are the rules of the legal game, and like any game, you can't play unless you know the basic rules. For example, "The judge hears the plaintiff's side of the case first," is a typical rule of procedure. Many courts will give you a free copy or summary of their procedural rules. You can usually get them from the clerk's office.

The second kind of law is the *substantive law*. These rules contain the *substance* of the law. Substantive rules define the rights of the parties in a particular situation. "When you pay for something, you have a right to receive something of value in exchange," "A home owner has a right to quiet enjoyment of his property," or "A vehicle making a left hand turn shall yield the right of way to oncoming traffic" are examples of substantive law.

When you go to the courthouse, you will find people who have special titles. The *clerk of court* or any *deputy clerk* is a person charged with keeping track of all the court papers, and scheduling hearings and trials. They also issue *subpoenas*, commanding witnesses to appear in court and bring with them whatever documents and items a party may request. each case is assigned a *case number, action number,* or *file number,* and is kept in its individual folder, or *file.* the person who makes sure the people are where they should be in the courthouse is the *bailiff.* a person who goes out to serve documents from the court may be called a *constable, marshal,* or *deputy sheriff.*

The judge can be called the *judge, magistrate, referee,* or *commissioner,* and is addressed as "Your honor," or simply, "Judge."

A *trial* is the formal airing of both sides of a legal dispute and the judge's final decision is the *judgment.*

In my judgment, that's all the terminology you'll need to know to handle your own small claims case and win.

PART II

JUST THE FACTS AND JUST THE LAW

Chapter 5

The Cause
of Action

Going to court for the first time is like standing over an untested diving spot. Even thinking about it makes many people weak in the knees. It doesn't have to be this way, if you know what to take with you when you jump.

Green grocers deal in vegetables. Courts deal in causes of action. In order to go to court to have a case heard, you need a cause of action. Once you have one, court personnel will immediately recognize it and you will be warmly received.

A legally sufficient cause of action has three elements. These are as follows:

1. A violation of a substantial right;

2. By someone who shouldn't have done it; and

3. Direct damage from the violation that can be measured in a specific dollar amount.

The facts that make up your complaint, your claim that someone has wronged you in some way, make up your cause of action. Your assertions that another person has violated a right you have in a particular way is what you bring with you to court. For example, your commercial relationship with the wrongdoer is broken (you trusted her and she swindled you!) and you want the court to fix it by increasing or restoring your bank balance at the wrongdoer's expense (you want your money back and some extra so she won't do this to anyone again).

But not all complaints you may have against others are sufficient for a court to hear. Certain hurts in life are unavoidable. It is expected of you to tolerate and live with some intrusions on your person, property, and peace. Even though they may make you cringe, hurt, or feel slightly sick, you are prevented from complaining in court about bad music, a child's icy drink that was accidentally spilled on you at a fast food restaurant, or cigar smoke in your face.

Most people have learned to withstand life's minor bumps and bruises. To survive in today's increasingly complex society, you need to develop a certain amount of emotional armor. In order to prevent frivolous law suits, the law presumes that people do have a reasonable measure of tolerance. This presumption is enforced by judges who promptly dismiss cases that have no merit and exist only to harass the accused. In many states, courts award money to the person sued on a claim that is frivolous or groundless.

Let's say you have a numbing headache every night when you come home from work because your job is so stressful. Or you just clobbered your thumb with the new 16-ounce hammer you bought at your corner hardware store. Or a part of your child's cereal box toy is missing. Or the brand of coffee you have enjoyed for years just doesn't taste right anymore.

Tough! These pains and complaints about them cannot be brought to court. They are not linked to a substantial violation of a recognized legal right. They are said to be *not actionable*. Law professors like to say that "for every wrong, there is a remedy." This is not quite true. It is more accurate to say, "If one of your recognized rights is substantially violated, and you can prove it, the law will give you a way to right the wrong." If you have a legal claim, what you are given is an *opportunity* to make it right. What you do with it is entirely up to you.

So, you must first have a complaint that is substantial. This does not necessarily mean that the wrong done has caused a large dollar loss to you.

Matters of Principle

The great majority of people who try their cases in small claims courts do it "for the principle of the matter." The greater the personal ethical principle involved in your case, the less the dollar amount involved needs to be. Let's look at an example.

John agreed to buy his friend Wade's TV for $20 down and $10 a week until the total price of $150 was paid. Delivery was due on full payment. John paid for three weeks, then he borrowed the rest of the money from his dad and called Wade to tell him that he would be stopping by to pay off the balance and pick up the TV. Wade replied, "Nah, I changed my mind." "Well, are you going to give me back my $50?"

"Nah," Wade said.

John can sue and win. Even in cases where the dollar value is less than this, if the violation is blatant, and the offender is stubborn about not doing right, you can sue and maintain your small claims suit against him. The principle "You should abide by your clear promises" has value in itself, and the courts will allow you to sue and recover for the breach of it. In these cases, it is not so much that the violation is monetarily substantial, but the principle is substantial and should be enforced in society. It encourages doing right. Each individual taking action to enforce these societal values keeps them viable in our culture.

While principle is important, it is not to be confused with spite. Suing your brother-in-law ("He really did it *this* time!") because he got paint splatters on the new ladder that he borrowed (something very typical of him) will not last long in court. Judges are quick to recognize lawsuits brought for spite and might deal with you in much the same way as the parent of a spiteful child.

Taking into account building and maintenance costs and salaries and benefits for all the court personnel, it costs taxpayers hundreds of dollars an hour to bring a case to trial and hold the trial. So although people's courts exist for small claims, consider curbing your urge to sue your dry cleaners over a ruined $8 tie.

Matters of Rights

Some rights you have that may have been violated to your damage may conflict with rights superior to yours: Constitutional rights. The Constitutional freedoms we enjoy come with a cost. Within limits, you can expect to hear obscenities from time to time; that is free speech. The unusual religious cultists who live in the house down the street may offend you, but their freedom to exist is tied to yours to worship as you wish. Business in your sandwich shop may be taking a temporary nose dive because there are pickets outside protesting the nude dance hall across the street, but you probably cannot recover your lost profits from the protesters.

You may not have a right to bring a court action in a case where your damage was due to an accident—a real accident, where no one is at fault. Accidents do happen, and there is often nobody to blame, except maybe yourself for being in that place at that time. Or you can always blame a higher authority.

If you are not sure if your claim will pass the "substantial" test in court, call the clerk's office in your local small claims court and ask if it is the kind of case that court will handle.

Is There Anyone Out There to Sue?

You may recall that a good cause of action requires someone who has done you wrong. Many "someones" have been known to disappear after the damage is done. If there is no one there to sue, you have no case. For instance, the potential defendant may be a person or corporation that you know is out of business or is in bankruptcy. Individual defendants may have left with no forwarding address or may have just been passing through town when you hired them to apply that "universal lifetime coating" on your driveway.

Small corporations can close their doors and go out of business one day and open the next day down the street with a new business identity. They do it all the time. Ordinarily, the debts and claims against the first business entity will not be chargeable to the second.

Finally, what if the wrongdoer is just plain broke? You may know beforehand that there is no cash, property, or other assets to satisfy your judgment if you win in court, and there is no realistic hope that there will be any in the future. If you sue and win, you may end up with the warm glow of satisfaction that you have fought a good legal fight and succeeded, but that's all.

If you do not have a cause of action, or someone solvent to sue, stop where you are, take a deep breath, exhale, and go do something fun. You must wait until another day to fight for your legal rights.

The Sum of All Rules

The law is simply the sum of all rules—constitutional provisions and the statutes of all governmental units: federal, state, county, and city. The law also includes judicial decisions interpreting the constitutions and statutes that govern our social and economic intercourse. It exists to secure the peace, order, and dignity in society. Laws exist to guide human conduct. Because the people who write the statutes have the impossible task of trying to identify and define human activity, which is limited only by the number of people in a society, these guidelines cannot apply clearly to every situation.

The Judge Rules: The Law of Your Case

The process of reaching a decision in a trial is simply deciding what a law means to the people in a single set of circumstances. In reaching this opinion, a judge or jury weighs what has been decided before in similar cases. The goal is to apply the law uniformly, and therefore fairly, to everyone. The decision of a judge or the verdict from a jury is what you get at the end of a trial. This decision declares that on that day, your rights are specifically established against your opponent, based on what you have convinced the judge or jury with regards to the facts of your case, and the law as the judge or jury understands it.

Although extreme human behavior is fodder for television talk shows and tabloid magazines, the range of human conduct fortunately does not often approach the extremes. So unless your case is unusual, the laws that govern your immediate legal problem have been long established and uniformly applied. Still, this is the real world and, ultimately, the law that is applicable to your case will be what the judge says it is. You have no choice but to assume that he or she knows it. When you point out all the reasons why you should win, if your argument makes sense and your facts are straight, the law will be applied in your favor. Don't worry about the marginal likelihood that the judge may not know what he or she is doing. Just get your facts straight and be as thorough as you can.

Here are some rules that can apply to countless everyday situations. One or more of these may apply to your case, and can provide you with guidance as to your legal claim. If the rule, when fairly applied, is not in your favor, it will still give you a more accurate view of the value of your case.

27 Rules You Can Use

1. If you get something of value, such as a place to live or the fruit of another's labor, you should pay for it.

2. Unless you are prevented from reading a document, and you sign it, you will be bound by what it says.

3. If you hurt a person or damage his or her property, you should pay for the injuries or damage.

4. Keep your promises.

5. You don't buy things to throw them in the trash bin. If you pay for something, you are entitled to get a useful value for your money.

6. There is no warranty on used goods unless the seller gives you one.

7. "As is" means "as is." (Imagine that!)

8. "Due by" means "due by." If you promised a payment on the first, it is late on the second. There is no "grace period," even when a late fee is not due until a later date.

9. Repair shops are not required to give warranties. They can still be held liable for work done negligently or intentionally wrong.

10. Business owners have a duty to keep their business premises reasonably safe for their customers.

11. Every person has a duty to act with that degree of care that is exercised by ordinarily prudent persons under the same or similar circumstances.

12. A person of sound mind is presumed to intend the natural and probable consequences of his acts.

13. An actual mistake cannot be the basis of a contract. You cannot form one if you are mistaken about its terms.

14. Accident means that the occurrence was not the result of intent or negligence on anyone's part.

15. An agent is a person who acts for another, the principal. A principal is liable for the acts of the agent for all acts the agent does within the scope of authority given to the agent.

16. If someone knowingly and willfully assumes a risk of injury to his person or property, he cannot hold another person responsible for the consequences.

17. You cannot complain about acts you consented to, as long as the consent is freely given, and not gotten by trickery.

18. To find the meaning of a contract, the first and most important question is, "What was the intention of the parties?"

19. A corporation is a distinct legal entity, separate from the people who own it and operate it.

20. A person can be held liable for the foreseeable consequences of her acts or omissions.

21. The fair market value of an item is the price it will bring when it is offered for sale by someone who doesn't have to sell it, and purchased by someone who wants it, but doesn't need it.

22. Every citizen has a right to enjoy his property and the sanctity of his person. Any act of another which substantially interferes with that enjoyment is a tort.

23. A sale consists of passing title from the seller to the buyer for a price.

24. A contract that no sane man would make, and no honest man would take advantage of, is not enforceable.

25. Words used in a contract bear their common meaning.

26. A gift is complete when the giver intends to give it, it is delivered, and the recipient gets it.

27. You deal with other people's property at your own risk.

The two rules that have the broadest application are number 4, "Keep your promises," which is the summation of all the law of contracts, and number 22, which summarizes all of tort law. If you carefully analyze your case in the light of these two principles of law, you should be able to fairly predict the outcome of your case at trial.

If you are ever in a law library, and feel awed by the number of thick and imposing books, the above is about all that is in there, said thousands of different ways, and applied to thousands of different case facts, each beginning with something gone wrong in the simple transactions encountered in daily life.

A court is a legal repair shop. Take your cause of action, your unique mixture of the facts and the law, to the courthouse seeking that your legal rights in your legal claim be adjusted in your favor. You will have your broken legal rights mended by showing the people there your specific problem, why you should win and what it will take to restore you from the injury of legal wrong.

CHAPTER 6

WHAT KIND of CLAIM DO YOU HAVE?

Every formal discipline—whether it is law, medicine, or publishing—has labels for the transactions that regularly occur in it. The law labels causes of action—the particular types of claims that are brought to court. These claims are distinguished by the differences in the rights that are affected, and the manner in which the particular claim arose.

In Chapter 4, we talked about the differences between procedural law and substantive law. Civil law, as opposed to criminal law, is divided into two broad categories: torts and contracts. These are matters of substantive law, the law that defines your rights in a particular situation.

Remember, these cases have been around since the beginning of time, so the principles of law governing these subjects are surprisingly uniform. Our whole system of laws came over with the Puritans in 1620, and the legislators who have written our modern day statutes and the courts that have interpreted them have consistently carried forward these age-old principles of law. They do not vary much from court to court or state to state, and because the society that came to be the United States has been on this continent for nearly 380 years, the customs that make up the "unwritten laws" this society runs on have been consistent, too. For example, "You don't take advantage of widows, orphans, the mentally, physically, or emotionally disadvantaged" is a widely accepted principle that can affect the outcome of any civil case.

There is one unwritten inflexible rule that underpins decisions in all courts in this country: "We will do our best to be fair to all parties." This should mean that everyone comes into court with an equal chance to prevail solely on the facts and laws pertaining to his or her case. The economic, social, educational, or other differences between people that have no bearing on the case should not be part of the trial. However, because *people* are making the decisions that result in judgments, errors can be made. Still, if the facts and circumstances of your case are very clear and the principles of law relating to them are well settled, you can expect that your facts and law will prevail. How heavily your judge will rely on fairness in deciding your case will derive from the peculiarities of your case and the judge's psychological makeup.

Judges are people with a strange job, but are first of all human. Each judge has unique biases and inclinations that color every judgment he or she makes. Often, they are not aware that these biases exist or affect their decisions. This shouldn't be a big worry, because the other side in your case will be subject to the same inclinations when the decision finalizing your case is rendered.

Like every life, every case is unique. Don't rely on what your brother-in-law or lawyer friend may tell you about the value of your case. Your case is unlike any other that has gone before it, and only you will best be able to predict the outcome of your trial, because you will know the most about it, and will know that you have prepared well.

Okay, so is your case a tort or contract case? Well, to determine that, we need to know the facts. What are facts, anyway? Facts are distinguished from, and different than, opinions or judgments. Facts can be verified by looking at some objective authority. Generally, opinions cannot. If I say, "Ted's dog bit me," I can show that it is true or false by looking at circumstances that can be measured by the senses. I have four holes in my forearm where the dog connected, and I have witnesses to the incident I can look to for verification.

On the other hand, if I say, "Ted is a jerk," I am reporting on my state of mind, a conclusion I have drawn about Ted. The best I can do to verify it is look around for people who have the same state of mind as me, who agree with me. There is no objective standard I can look to for verification. This judgment summing up Ted's character is an opinion.

The process of proving facts in court is known as presenting your evidence. *Proof* is any matter that tends to sway the mind toward believing or disbelieving the truth or falsity of a claim. The witnesses we bring to court are the verifying authorities, and other evidence we bring to court, such as documents, photographs, and recordings are used to show that what you claim happened is fact.

The difference between facts and opinions is important, because what you bring to court should be the facts. What you want is an opinion about your facts that is in your favor. You accomplish this by persuading the judge that you deserve to win. You are asking the judge to consider facts A, plus B, plus C (the applicable law) and conclude: You are entitled to win, and you do win. This is the opinion you are looking for when you present a case at trial.

Your opinion about what happened doesn't matter at all. Only the judge's opinion counts. Even if everyone in the world and elsewhere thinks that Ted is a jerk, if Ted has the facts and law on his side, he will win.

People who are passionate about their causes want the judge to know every possible bad thing they know about the person who is opposing them in court. That you think the other party is a crook, liar, or mangy dog is not really about them, but about the reaction they have caused inside you, and it does not matter when you are trying to get money that party owes you.

The facts we find in civil cases deal with claimed violations of *private wrongs* or *civil wrongs*. Again, crimes are violations by an individual affecting the society as a whole, and are defined by the penal statutes. If you violate a criminal statute, you are to be punished by the government whose law you broke. The fine money goes to the same place, and the government also foots the bill for jail, should that be your punishment.

Private wrongs, also called *civil wrongs,* arise from the violation of some duty imposed by civil laws or by agreement. They are enforced by civil lawsuits. If you have been wronged and recover, the other side is not punished. The extent of their loss, if any, is only to the extent of what you win. The purpose of the civil lawsuit is to put the parties back into the same position they would have been in if the wrong had not occurred. Because it is impossible in many of these cases to undo the wrongs, money is substituted for the value of the harm done.

It is important that you understand the nature of your claim. Once you decide that your problem is a contract problem, you can apply an analysis to it that will prepare your case for trial. You need to prove different points for contracts than for torts, and you defend against these claims in different ways. Once you name your cause, courthouse personnel will better be able to help you, too.

In your opening statement, if you can say, "Your honor, this case involves the tort of conversion," everyone will be impressed, except the opposition, who will be downright scared. So be sure you know what your claim is before you go to small claims court.

CHAPTER 7

TORTS:
THE HURTS
WE SUFFER

A tort is a civil wrong that occurs without the existence of a contract between the actor and victim. "Tort" comes from the Latin word meaning "to twist" and is related to "torture." Torts are injuries to your person or property. They are violations of a *duty* imposed on people by general law applicable in a particular set of circumstances.

To prove a tort in court, you need to show three things:

1. There is a legal duty in the subject matter for the other person to act or not act in a certain way.
2. The duty was breached or violated.
3. You suffered damage as the direct result of the breach or violation.

For example, under general principles of law, manufacturers have a duty to make sure their products are safe when they reach the marketplace. Poison in pills and cigar butts in soda cans are not acceptable. Similarly, you have the general right to be free to operate your business without unreasonable interference, to be free from significant physical and emotional pain caused by others, and to be free to have your personal property and real estate not interfered with or damaged in any significant way by others, and the right not to be hoodwinked by unscrupulous dealings that result in damage to you. When you do not have a contract with the person who harmed you, you have a tort.

Your private rights to be free from harm can be violated in two ways: intentionally or negligently. (You can also be hurt accidentally, but accidents are not *causes of action*.)

The law presumes that people intend the natural consequences of willful acts. When they harm someone intentionally, they mean it; when they do it negligently, it is because they aren't as careful as the law requires.

Let's take a look at an example of a violation caused by negligence. Bronson liked to shop. One afternoon she was browsing in her favorite department store, and as she came around the end of a tall shelf stacked with outdoor goods, a five-gallon plastic cooler fell off the top shelf and hit her in the face, knocking out her front teeth. On the other side of the aisle, a young man was stocking this upper shelf with still more coolers, even as Bronson hollered and he heard the cooler hit the floor.

He didn't try to hurt her. His act was not intentional, but this employee had failed in the store's duty to keep its customers reasonably safe from injury. He wasn't as careful as he should have been and it directly caused injury. This same duty can be violated in many different ways, such as a store's failure to clean up a spill or allowing rainwater to make the floor slippery.

The difference between intentional and negligent torts is the same as between Nasty Neighbor and Inattentive Adjoining Landowner. When Nasty sprayed that herbicide to kill everything on his side of the line, he purposefully gave a few squirts onto your Japanese flowering crabapple tree. Inattentive Adjoining Landowner sprayed some of the same stuff along your mutual property line and didn't notice that his land was uphill from yours. The flowering tree was doomed in the next rain. The private right that was violated is the right to have your property free from injury at the hands of another. Just like the case arising in stores, violations of this right can arise in circumstances limited only by your imagination.

Whether intentional or not, the effect is the same. If you can show the duty, breach, and direct damage, you have the right to be in court saying "Tort!"

Types of Torts

Whether intentional or not, torts have their own labels, depending on the individual right that is violated.

Tort actions complaining about injuries to one's person are common in small claims courts. They claim a violation of the right to have yourself free from intentional or negligent hurts at the hands of other people or the instruments they control. In the cases of negligence, the injury is caused by instruments or agents the wrongdoer should have controlled, but didn't. These two, intentional and negligent, are known collectively as *personal injury claims*.

If someone takes his hands, feet, or other weapon to you and causes injury, it is a matter of intentional *assault and battery*. These also may be the subject of criminal prosecution, which will be discussed later.

Almost any kind of agent or instrumentality that people are supposed to keep under control can be the cause of a personal injury—dog bites, cat scratches and horse nips, for instance. Others in and endless list of possibilities include children's toys left where they should not be, such as on front sidewalks; foreign objects and defective structures in places of business, such as a display case with sharp edges, or fishing lures displayed without the hooks being covered; store displays that topple over; and car doors unexpectedly swinging open as you pass by in the parking lot.

There are a few cases that fall into a special niche in this area of tortious activity, called *attractive nuisances*. A person who maintains a structure or object that is peculiarly attractive to others, especially children, is required to be extra careful to prevent injuries from it. Damages follow when injuries result from an unattended ladder propped against a house, electric start lawn tractors, and unfenced or unwatched swimming pools of all types and sizes.

The tort called *trespass* encompasses all damages done, intentionally or negligently, to your property. Historically, injuries done to you or any interest in your real estate or personal property were called trespass, but the term has become increasingly narrower in meaning. Now it is limited to damage to real estate and the buildings on them.

Trespass can take the form of an injury to your right to occupy your property. When a neighbor intentionally or without regard to the facts, constructs his dog run, fence, or even part of his garage on your side of the property line, you can recover for the destruction of your azaleas by the dog run, for the cost of tearing down the fence if he won't, or even the value of that small portion of your real estate that is now covered by his garage. It could be the damage done by a teenager riding a bike on your front lawn.

Home improvements often cause small disasters for neighbors. For example, the tree surgeon's truck can crack your driveway or take out a small tree; the falling tree might take a long stretch of your gutter to the ground or level part of your hedge by mistake; your neighbor's plumber may deposit excess dirt on the other side of the property line and leave it. Even otherwise neighborly clean-up activities might cause damages. Water from a hose left on overnight can be the cause of a trespass tort. A baseball accidently thrown through your window by a group of neighborhood children is a cause for a trespass tort.

All of these, and many more situations, constitute trespass. In each, the person who caused the injury of allowed it to occur had a duty to control his instrument, agent or activity, and the failure caused compensable injury. The following elements constitute what you must prove to recover damages in these cases:

1. The duty.
2. The lapse or breach of the duty.
3. The directly resulting harm.

I mentioned attractive nuisances when discussing personal injuries previously. Your right to the "peaceful enjoyment" of your house or home can also be wrongfully invaded by annoyances or disturbances from next door or nearby. These are known as just plain old *nuisances*. These are offenses to your senses. They may potentially be damaging to your health or to the community standard of decency. Smoke from constantly burning trash piles, excessive party noise, or chemical smells can make up a claim for a nuisance. You can get money to assuage your assaulted senses to the extent of your provable injuries.

In small claims court, what you can usually get is money. Most of the time, your main concern will be to have the nuisance stopped. So you will need to go to a court that has the power to order it stopped. You will be able to recover all provable damages incurred up to the time the nuisance is stopped in that court, too. Ask the clerk in your local small claims court if the judge has the authority to abate a nuisance for you.

Intentional or negligent injuries to property other than those connected to real estate are proven the same way. If your car is bumped by another car in a parking lot, if your wedding gown is ruined by an inept waiter, or if your living room rug is damaged by a salesperson selling "the greatest cleaning discovery ever," you can sue. And you can win.

There are injuries to other recognizable rights that are not as common. For example, your right to personal liberty and freedom can be violated when someone with no authority detains you without your consent. These cases can arise when a store prevents all customers from leaving because a suspected shoplifter is in the store, or if someone without cause tries to make a "citizen's arrest" on you, or even grabs your arm preventing you from leaving. Remember two things about these types of cases: You must be able to prove that you were actually injured. Even if you were only "mortified," you may still have a provable case if a psychologist or other mental health professional will testify that you were in fact injured, and how the injury affected your life.

You also have a right to be free from intentional psychological damage. If some evildoer falsely tells you that your child has been seriously injured, you can recover for your resulting emotional injury. Again, proof of psychological damage would be the same as in false arrest or imprisonment cases.

You and your rights to operate a business are protected from false damaging statements which constitute *libel* and *slander*. If you discover that a competitor is falsely telling your customers that the drinks you sell are watered down and you can prove that you lost a specific amount of business as the direct result, you can recover. If all else is equal, you can prove it by comparing the business books from before and after the statements were made.

How much is this special damage to your psyche worth? In most cases, you need to prove the value of your damages with some specificity. But in these personal injury cases, where the injury is to your physical or emotional well-being, peace, or feelings, the value, once you describe what happened and how it affected you, is up to the "enlightened conscience" of the judge or jury, taking into consideration all the circumstances and treating each party fairly. Damages that are not certain because of their subjective nature (how do you measure pain and suffering, for example?) are known as *unliquidated damages*. Because this is true, there is some risk of these cases having a value greater than the small claims court you are in can handle. Once you know the top dollar amount your local court can deal with, you can make a decision to bring it there or to a different court that can hear cases involving larger dollar amounts.

Further, if your injury or medical treatment is complicated, your case may need a doctor's testimony about your treatment and condition. Your doctor would be the best witness to testify that your injury was caused by the wrong done to you by the other party, and that the treatment was reasonable and necessary. You may need an attorney to secure this testimony for you in the proper form. All personal injury cases where there is a question that you might be entitled to more money than your small claims court can award should be pursued in other "bigger money" courts.

Chapter 8

Contracts: The Promises We Make

By far, most small claims cases arise from contracts. Contracts are the promises we live by, the grist for the mill of commerce, the oil for its wheels. There are two kinds of promises that are tested in contract disputes, express and implied. We make express promises by putting our intentions into language. Alternately, we imply promises by our actions. In some cases, implied promises may be imposed on us by rules that have arisen over centuries of commerce. For example, people generally expect that a worker who holds himself out to the public as a professional will do professional quality work. The law upholds these implied promises as strongly as those that are spoken or written.

The express promises we make are easy to spot. For example, Clarke promises to pay Tanner $200 for her used lawn tractor, and Tanner promises to deliver the tractor when she gets Clarke's cash. The same kind of promises, oral or written, comprise transactions as simple as the deal between Clarke and Tanner and as complex as the merger of two major corporations.

The promises we make that are implied from our actions are harder to identify, but make sense in a complex commercial world. Implied promises are those that arise because the transactions we make are so common that there is no need to express them, or such promises as will be supplied by the law to keep our transactions moving and fair.

When you put bills or coins in a vending machine, the candy supplier has made a promise that when you press the button, your choice will come out. The supplier of that candy bar has made a promise, or the laws require the promise, that what you get will be wholesome, edible, and without dead insects inside.

Unless someone is clearly a volunteer, the law will provide a promise to pay him or her for work undertaken and done with an acceptable level of skill. Similarly, the law will supply an implied promise to pay for lodgings at a reasonable rate, even where there is no lease or even an informal agreement. This is true even when the landlord is not in the business of renting out property.

The law presumes that when you give someone else something valuable—your labor, a concert ticket, or a night's shelter—you expect something of value in return. The contrary—that you volunteered your labor, that the ticket or lodging was a gift—needs to be shown clearly to overcome this assumption.

These implied promises supplied by the law get clearer in business situations. You are required to pay for restaurant meals and bus and taxi rides because the law says that when you eat the food or take the ride, you implicitly promise to pay for it at the regular rate. These promises that are supplied by the law are necessary to keep commerce going. They support and further the reasonable expectations of the parties to these transactions.

Of the thousands of promises we make and receive in our lifetimes, almost all are fulfilled without our even noticing them. We do begin to notice them, though, when something goes wrong. The whole area of domestic relations law, for example, depends on what goes wrong with the marriage contract.

Contracts result from the exchange of promises about some particular subject matter. The idea of an exchange of promises is important, because many of the promises we make—a promise to take out the garbage, make some telephone calls for a church committee, or "to love you forever"—do not involve this exchange, and so do not result in enforceable contracts.

The exchange of promises can be of money for goods, such as what happens during your weekly trip to the grocery store. It can also be goods for goods (such as in a traditional barter), money or property for services, or any combination of these.

The exact wording of promises can be as different as the people who make them. So, each contract will either be enforceable or not on its own terms. This is one reason you should not rely on what happened in your brother-in-law Filbert's case.

If you have an exchange of promises, and both parties 1) are clear about what they promised and have told the other party clearly what the promise is, and 2) they understand what the other party has promised, it is likely that you have entered into an enforceable agreement. The test of any contract is : Has there been a "meeting of the minds" as to the subject matter of the contract? The more specific you are about the manner in which the agreement is to be carried out, the time of performance, and/or the method of payment, the more likely it is that you have an enforceable agreement.

Not every exchange of promises results in an enforceable contract. The subject matter may be trivial ("For two cents, I'll run naked through Central Park"), or illegal ("I'll give you $50 if you will steal a new car stereo for me"). This relates to the discussion earlier about real, substantial causes of action that courts will recognize and resolve at trial.

While this rarely comes up, sometimes a person makes a promise and does not have the legal capacity to keep it. A contract with a child, anyone who is under the age of majority in your state, will ordinarily not be enforceable until after he or she reaches that age, usually 18. Banks now routinely issue credit cards to 16 and 17 year olds. The children build up big balances, and the credit card companies wait until they are 18 years old to try to collect, knowing they cannot collect as long as the kids are underage. The banks are taking some risk, because the law in most states allows the kids to disavow these debts upon reaching the age of 18. They did not have the legal capacity to make the contract to pay the debts accumulated by the card when they were minors, and now that they are adults, they can choose to reject the credit or the responsibility.

If you enter into a contract with someone who has not reached the age of majority, you do it at your own risk. This is becoming more common as children have access to more money at an earlier age.

Insane persons and those who are voluntarily or involuntarily markedly under the influence of alcohol or other drugs fall into this category, too. They are not able to contract with anyone.

Oral contracts are just as enforceable as written contracts. Assuming both parties are able to enter into a contract and there has been a "meeting of the minds," for most cases, it doesn't matter if your contract is in writing or just spoken or implied between the parties. I recently read a news story about a producer winning a multimillion-dollar judgment against an actress based on her violation of an oral contract.

The problem with oral contracts is that they are very hard to prove. What you have in your mind about what was promised may not be as certain as you would like it to be, and later on may be shaded by what actually happened when it was time to carry out the contract. Things may have come up that you never anticipated when you first made the agreement. They can result in "swearing contests" at trial, where one party swears the contract was one thing and the other side swears it was another, and the judge must choose whom to believe.

People make oral contracts all the time. Ours used to be a handshake society. Complex business deals were finalized on the basis of a handshake, and details were worked out later. Many people think commerce still runs this way. Not too long ago, a single mother of two appeared in my courtroom claiming that she had been taken advantage of by a home remodeling contractor. When their dealings began, she gave him a handwritten list of 12 instructions, most of which were described in a few words, such as, "Tear out kitchen walls." Over the following six months, she paid him more than $24,000, with no invoices or receipts for materials or labor. She thought "maybe" she had been taken advantage of.

The deal made on a handshake has not been a wise course to take since about 1860, when legal cases first started to be reported in this country. By far, one of the hardest things a judge does when deciding if there is a contract, is to try to find out what was in the minds of the parties when those minds were supposed to have "met."

Along with testifying about what terms you understand are in your oral contract, you can prove it by presenting any writings that relate to the contract and by testimony about how the parties acted after the agreement was entered. But people's actions and vague writings are subject to many interpretations. If you have an oral contract, and there exist *any* writings, memoranda, notes, photographs, drawings, or anything else tangible that could be examined to see what you agreed on, get it together. You may have a chance to show it and explain it to the judge. Contracts that are partially oral and partially written are classified as oral contracts.

Because as a judge I have an obligation to educate the public when I can, on a weekly basis I recite one of the greatest rules of law ever devised by man. It is known locally as the

"Paper Sack Rule": *If you have an agreement, and there is a paper sack on the ground near you, pick it up and write your agreement on it.*

This is especially important and helpful in service contracts. From the shade tree mechanic, whose contract consists of a soiled Work Order form purchased at the local business supply, to the multi-thousand dollar renovation project you have on your home, get it in writing if you can. If your contract is oral, what you must prove are the same things you would have put into your written contract if you had one.

One last note on types of contracts. Some contracts *must* be in writing to be enforceable. State law determines which ones. Most states have adopted a Statute of Frauds in some form, named after the English statute of 1677. They require that to be enforceable, certain contracts must be in writing and signed by the person who should perform what is stated in the contract. They exist to prevent fraud or trickery in areas where ordinary citizens might easily be fooled. Real estate sales, employment, and other contracts that may not be performed in a year as well as prenuptial agreements are typical. If there is any question that your contract may fall into one of these categories, you can call the court clerk or call an attorney to discuss it for free, as explained in Chapter 11.

To win your case for any contract, you must show:

1. That there was a meeting of the minds, a basic understanding of the agreement between the parties.
2. What the terms of the agreement were, the time, place, and manner of performance, and when it was supposed to be completed.
3. That the other party broke its promise (breached the contract).
4. That you were damaged in a particular amount because of the broken promise.

For defendants, if any one of these elements is not or cannot be proven, you win.

For either side, plaintiff or defendant, to help you decide how strong your case may be, ask yourself:

1. What is *your* understanding of the agreement? What should have happened?
2. Did everyone act the way you expected them to? Actions still speak louder than words. Because the precise meanings in most contracts are assumed (you wouldn't care if the carpenter you hired drove nails right- or left-handedly) or implied, the judge will especially want to know what people did about it. People mostly act in an intentional manner, especially when they have some expectation about how it will affect them later on. So even though there may not be a written or "formal" agreement, the judge can find one based on what everybody did to further the enterprise. The parties and witnesses can testify to what happened.
3. Is there any evidence of the agreement besides what the witnesses say? If there is *anything* written, look at it—a repair order or laundry claim ticket, any notes taken during a telephone conversation, any letters written or exchanged in the middle of the contract, handwritten bills, or drawings of how a project was supposed to look.

Prior agreements about similar transactions will tend to fill in the blanks concerning the intention about the newer ones. If you have transacted business repeatedly with another and established a fixed pattern of dealing with the person, an implied agreement can be found based on this course of dealing.

4. How did the other party fail to live up to the promises made to you? There may have been more than one way. For example: "Not only did he not paint my house the color I wanted, but he painted it in a two-tone version of the wrong colors! Then he billed me twice the estimate."

5. How much did you lose as the direct result of the failure(s)? You need to be able to show how much you lost because of your failed expectations. If you paid for something that was worthless, you should be able to recover the purchase price. If you had to pay, for example, a second plumber to fix a first plumber's botched job, you should ask for what you paid the second plumber to complete the work. This is true even though you may have had to pay the second plumber more. You have a right to the full benefit of your bargain.

    Look at the financial position you were in before you entered into the contract. If you win, the judge should put you back into that position as closely as possible, as if the bad contract had never occurred.

    If your property was damaged beyond repair, you may be able to recover its full value at the time it was damaged. Not replacement value, but fair market value at the time the damage was done. Once you have used something, it is not worth what it was new. A car salesman once told me that the minute you drive a car off the lot, it depreciates 25 percent in value. But if you show that you purchased your mink coat for $3,500, for example, and wore it only three times before the dry cleaner misplaced it, you should be able to get close to the full value, as if it were new. If you wore it 20 times, it would be helpful for you to be able to place a specific value on it at its depreciated value. If you expected to wear it 200 times over the life of the coat, it would be depreciated 10 percent. You should recover $3,150 for its loss. You can be creative in your demands and proof of your damages, as long as you are reasonable. The judge must have a "reasonable basis" to award you a specific sum of money.

Defendants, if you are sued on a contract and do not agree with the plaintiff's point of view (and who would expect you to?), you can assert several defenses to prevent having the contract enforced against you. Here, too, a strong defense is your best offense. Assert one of these successfully and it will do away with the plaintiff's claim.

1. There was no agreement. Contracts do not exist at all if there is no meeting of the minds as to any part of the proposed agreement. For example, no rate of pay or contract price, no description of what each of you will do for the other, or no exchange of promises at all, actual or implied. You are saying, "I never agreed with the plaintiff about this at all!" You may have had negotiations preliminary to making an agreement, but no accord was reached.

2. There was an agreement, but it was different than the one the plaintiff claims existed. Show by testimony and other evidence what the real agreement was.

3. You did not violate the contract. Or if you did a little, the plaintiff disregarded it altogether.

4. There was a contract, but you entered into it by mistake. If you had known what the true facts were, not your mistaken ones, you never would have entered into the contract in the first place. So, it is unfair that you be bound by it.

5. There was a contract, but you were lured into accepting it by deception and trickery. Therefore, you should not be bound by it.

6. There was a contract, but:

   A. Before it started, you and the plaintiff changed your minds and agreed to different terms.

   B. Before it started, you and the plaintiff agreed not to go forward with it.

   C. After it began, you and the plaintiff agreed to different terms and a new contract.

   D. You or the plaintiff acted totally different than you had originally agreed. Your contract was changed by actions that were not accepted by one of the parties to the agreement.

7. You had a contract and you broke your promises, but the plaintiff wasn't damaged in nearly the amount he or she claims.

8. There were two contracts. The second one changed everything.

9. There was a contract, but it required one of you to do something illegal or immoral. Therefore, you cannot be bound by it.

10. There was a contract, but it became impossible to perform. Something unforeseen happened, making the contract impossible or worthless. For example, you agreed to paint the plaintiff's house, but then before the job began, the house burned down.

11. There was a contract, but you didn't have to do anything under the agreement until the plaintiff did something first, and he or she never did it. In this one, there is a condition that must be met before the other party is required to perform his or her promise. You might argue successfully with this defense: "Yes, I agreed to paint the plaintiff's house as soon as he got the paint. He never did."

12. There was a contract, but when it came time for you to perform, the plaintiff said you did not have to. Your performance was excused.

Not all cases arising from contracts that come to small claims court have to do with the agreements themselves. Some are disputes about what is supposed to happen after the contract is completed. This takes us into the world of *warranties*—promises made after the work is done. Simply, a warranty is a promise to stand by one's work. The person who gives it is saying, "My work is good. If you find anything wrong with it, in the next 30 (60, 90) days, then I will make it right." Like the promises that make up contracts, warranties can be express or implied, written or oral. Some are supplied by the law.

In all states in this country, new goods have warranties that go with them when they are sold. There are also federal statutes, the most well-known being the Magnuson-Moss Warranty Act, that apply to all states. These are controlled by state statutes that grant different warranty rights. You may have heard of a "Lemon Law" for new cars, a recent addition to the warranty laws in many states. If you want to know specifically what warranty rights are given to you in your state by law, you can call the consumer affairs office of the secretary of state's office, or any consumer rights organization in your state.

Within the bounds of applicable law, the warranties that you get from a manufacturer can be limited to specific areas of the product and for specific times. When you get a "limited six-year or 60,000-mile power train warranty," it means that this warranty does not cover anything on the car except the power train. "Limited" is the most important word in this warranty. You will not find out what the limitation is unless you read the *very* fine print in your owner's manual. Warranties on other products appear on the package or in those package inserts we so casually throw away.

New things you buy should work. If an item does not, take it back to the place where you bought it. Do this even if the package insert says, after you retrieve it and uncrumple it, that you must return the goods to the manufacturer.

Most of the time, the merchant will exchange the item for the same model that does work, or refund your money. They do this for two reasons: The law probably requires it, and they do not want to get a reputation in the community for selling shoddy goods. Most merchants care about their reputations in the business community. Those who do not usually do not stay in business very long.

If the merchant refuses to give you an exchange or refund, before you sue, make that call to your local or state consumer affairs office for direction. If you still get no satisfaction, you can sue the seller for your lost purchase price. Remember, the contract is between you and the merchant. You promised to pay money for the goods. He or she promised to give you goods for your money. The warranties that attach are additional promises that the articles will, in fact, be good. You can sue and receive your provable damages if the goods do not meet a reasonable standard of quality.

One caution: If you have a warranty, you must let the merchant try to make it good before you sue. You cannot just throw up your arms in disgust and sue the person for everything he or she's got, though this may be your first strong inclination. If the law gives you a warranty, or secures its enforcement, the law will also place a duty on you to try to first cure the problem yourself.

Warranties on used merchandise are a different story. Unless you received an express warranty (the best kind is in writing), you probably do not have the legal right to complain if the used goods do not work. You can always complain, but you will not have the right to have a court adjust your situation to your satisfaction. Without an express warranty on used goods, you probably do not have a cause of action if they are defective.

The harder cases to win are those where nothing is said about the quality of the goods or what is to happen if the buyer is not satisfied.

For example, Hartley sold his old friend Ahearn his well-used, well-worn riding lawn mower for $100. The only thing Hartley said was, "It works fine." Ahearn loaded it onto his pickup truck, took it home, and used it. It worked fine for 20 minutes, and then ground to a howling stop. It was a short ride. Ahearn thought that *he* had been taken for a ride. Hartley argued that his friend knew how old the machine was when he bought it, and that he could tell just by looking at it that the mower was used—very used.

Ahearn lost in my court because there was no warranty given by Hartley. This seller made no promise, express or implied, that the machine would work for 10 minutes, a week, a year, or any time beyond the moment of the sale. There was no evidence that Hartley knew that there was anything wrong with the mower when he sold it. Ahearn lost his $100. Both of them lost a 30-year friendship. This happens often in matters of principle. It doesn't seem worth it sometimes. Weigh this when considering whether you want to pursue a claim or settle one you have started. Money is just a medium of exchange. Property can be replaced. Friendship can't.

Problems with warranties show up in service contracts all the time. In service contracts, one person promises to pay money to another to perform a service. The person who is to perform the service promises to do so in exchange for the money.

Quackenbush was a penny-pincher. He wanted his Porsche fixed cheap. He mostly wanted to avoid the $1,200 cost he had been quoted by a dealer for the work he needed done. A co-worker told him about a great mechanic, Shadetree, whose specialty was fixing Porsches evenings and weekends in the barn behind his house. Shadetree's main job was as a professional musician. Quackenbush gave Shadetree $350 to fix the clutch in the Porsche.

He fixed it, but 10 days later, the clutch burned up. So did Quackenbush.

Quackenbush lost his case in small claims court. Shadetree didn't give any kind of warranty, oral or written, promising his work would last. Considering that Quackenbush knew that Shadetree was not in the auto repair business, and considering what he paid for the job, it looked like he got what he paid for. If Shadetree had been in the auto repair business and had held himself out to the general public as a professional, the judge may have found that his workmanship should be held to a reasonably professional standard, that his work should have lasted more than 10 days. The judge then would have imposed a warranty on him to that extent. This is an example of a warranty that may have been imposed by the law, even though the parties were silent about it.

Had Shadetree said, "I'll guarantee my work for 30 days," or written it out or had it printed on the bottom of a Work Order form, Quackenbush would have left the courthouse a much happier man.

If you buy anything marked "as is," you really are buying it "as is," with all the defects you could have discovered if you had given it a reasonable inspection. Let's say you buy a used car "as is," and you have not been prevented from fully inspecting it or from having your mechanic check it. If you drive 15 feet and all four doors fall off, stop. Go back and pick up your doors, for they are yours, along with the rest of your drafty purchase, or you could be charged with littering.

If it is "as is," the car is yours, even if you are still making payments on it.

Not long ago, Mrs. Welby decided to buy her teenage son a used car. She was looking for a particular Japanese brand because of its reputation for going 200,000 to 300,000 miles before becoming irreparable. Mr. Farcas had two of them in his front yard. She bought the orange one. It died almost immediately. When the case came to court, Farcas and Welby agreed that he had given her the opportunity to have the car inspected by her mechanic before she bought it. She didn't "get around to it" until the day after she paid for the car, when Mr. Farcas gave her the bill of sale that said, "This vehicle is sold *as is*, without warranties." Farcas even pointed this language out to her when he gave her the bill of sale.

When Mrs. Welby's mechanic checked the car over the next day, he noticed a lot of hoses and wires that didn't go anywhere. Although he was an experienced mechanic, he could not identify the manufacturer of the motor. Mrs. Welby wanted her money back! She did not get it. Her purchase was "as is."

One fact that helped Mr. Farcas was that he was not in the used car business, so a duty to inspect or to know what he was selling could not be imposed on him. Even had he been in car sales, the "as is" on the bill of sale would have doomed Mrs. Welby's case.

Automobile salespeople and others who regularly deal in used goods are notorious for saying things such as, "This is a great car," "It is good, reliable transportation," "This is sure to give you years of good service," or "This car (boat, stereo, motorcycle, television, computer, camera, bicycle, watchdog) is for you!" These statements and those like them say nothing specific about the quality of the goods you are about to buy. If they are promises about the future, because no one knows what will happen in the future, the promises cannot be enforced against the speaker. These are known in the sales world as *puffing*. Good salespeople are expected to emphasize the good attributes of what they sell and minimize the shortcomings. They puff their goods up in the eyes of the prospective buyer, making them look larger, better, and more valuable than they would appear from a more evenhanded examination. Expect to be puffed at and accept these exaggerations for what they are. Don't take them seriously. The law doesn't.

If you take a minute to reread the previous puffing statements, you can see that what they assert are matters of opinion. Because they are not statements of fact, they cannot be the basis for a claim of fraud, deception, trickery, or misrepresentation.

Suppose a salesman says, "This car has had one previous owner, a retired schoolteacher who drove it only to church on Sunday and to her Thursday night bridge game, and it has only 20,000 miles on it." If the salesman knows that he bought it from the local police agency after its having been used by a drug ring to run drugs between Canada and Mexico, and in fact has 220,000 miles on it, there is deception you can sue on. Misrepresentations of facts result in fraud, discussed later in greater detail. They can appear in many ways, in contracts for both new and used goods and in contracts for services. Ads for goods may contain facts that are blatantly not true or merely half-truths. A house painter may grossly overstate his qualifications and experience. You may pay $3,000 cash for a used truck on the implied representation that the seller has title to it when h doesn't. A mortgage lender may take a fee up front from you on the representation that he has the contacts to get you a loan, but then he does nothing. A roofer may get $400 from you for "materials," but never materializes himself. (Unlike promises about the future, these last two examples show a present intention not to perform, an intent to deceive at the time the transaction is entered into.)

Be aware that the law frowns on any kind of deception, and if you are defrauded, you may recover additional damages in your civil case to punish the wrongdoer and to prevent him from repeating his wrongful conduct. Some fraud is criminal, and you have other ways to get your money back. This will be discussed further in Chapter 11. But as long as a seller, professional or not, did not misrepresent facts about an item you bought as is, you've lost if the item turns out to be trash.

One final note on contracts: The laws concerning certain special contracts, such as landlord and tenant, the collection of judgments from other states, securities law, and foreclosures on personal property vary from state to state. The laws in these areas have developed to meet the peculiar conditions in your state. For example, in a rural state, the law may favor landlords, while in an urban state, it may favor tenants.

If your case is about one of these, you need to ask a few more questions when you are gathering information for your case. Sources and suggestions are given in Chapter 12.

CHAPTER 9

CONTRACT CASES: PROMISES OTHERS HAVE MADE

These cases are true. The names and minor facts have been changed to protect the egos of real people. They are presented not so much in the hope that your case will be exactly like one of them, but to show you how real life situations play out in small claims trials.

The Case of "Honey, the Floor Is Shrinking!"

One bright Saturday morning, Ella Johnson looked across her kitchen at her husband, Sims, screwed her face into a very crooked frown, and said, "We need a new floor." (Meaning: "I want a new floor and we are going to have one.")

Ella took the smart route: She visited three carpet and floor covering stores, picked up and actually read brochures about the quality and characteristics of different products, and decided on an upper-middle-grade vinyl, made to go over their existing floor. At the end of the manufacturer's brochure, it said, not too conspicuously, "Unless properly applied, may shrink up to one percent over time." Then Ella started making calls to find someone to do the work.

Pendley, the owner of "Floor Mania," got the job. This was after he told the Johnsons that he had years of experience (actually, half a year's) with all the available products, and that he had done "scads" of floor replacement jobs just like theirs. Price: $1,200; warranty: "I have never had a problem with this flooring. You won't either."

On installation day, Pendley took the stove and refrigerator out of the kitchen. He then noticed that the old floor was not stuck to the plywood underneath. The glue had all dried out, and the old floor just lifted off. "This has got to go," he declared to himself.

With the Johnson's permission, he took it up, cut it up, and loaded it into his old Ford Econoline van. He then put the new floor down, got his check, and left.

Except for a few minor bumps, the Johnson's new floor looked great! For a while.

Early one morning, the slanted rays of sunlight hit the corner of the floor just right. Ella looked but wasn't quite sure. It looked like the floor was retreating from the wall in the corner. Yes, there was definitely a white strip where the plywood was showing—about 1/8" from the lower edge of the molding. She thought, "That's okay. Just hadn't noticed it before."

The next week, she found herself in the same corner. Sure enough, the space between the wall and the flooring was growing. Her floor was shrinking! On her hands and knees now, she could see that the few bumps had grown, and were still growing! And there was a raised blotch where a puddle of glue had been covered up...and there was a four-foot edge of plywood subfloor that had raised up. As she examined all around the edge, she could see that it was all getting smaller. She imagined that at this rate, within a few weeks, all she would have would be a spot of new floor in the middle of her kitchen, about one yard square.

The Johnsons decided to sue. From that day until trial day, they got madder and madder, as they lived with a kitchen floor that seemed to be shrinking under their feet. They sued Pendley for their $1,200, plus $300 for the old floor that he threw away.

At trial, Pendley testified, "You knew this floor would shrink. It's the manufacturer's fault. You told me it was okay to cut up the old floor and throw it out, even though you knew the new floor was made to go over the old floor. The job I did was up to acceptable standards."

The Johnsons argued, "We didn't get what we paid for. He said we wouldn't have any trouble. He is the professional and should have known better."

After hearing testimony from both sides and looking at the other evidence—pictures of the floor, Pendley's "order form" with the very small print in the lower left-hand corner that read, "All warranties are the manufacturer's," the canceled check brought by the Johnsons, and the manufacturer's brochure brought by Pendley—the judge awarded the angry Johnsons a judgment for $1,200.

The rules and reasons the judge used:

1. You don't buy something to throw it in the trash.

2. When two parties contract, the one with more knowledge and expertise about the subject of the contract should know and avoid foreseeable problems. Pendley knew from experience, or should have known, that this floor was made to go over an existing floor, not the plywood underlayment. It was Pendley's responsibility.

3. When consumers buy new goods and have them professionally installed, they have a right to rely on the expert's professional abilities.

4. A newly installed floor with bumps, grooves, and plateaus is not acceptable.

5. A contract, here Pendley's order form, will be construed against the drafter, or the party who presents it. Pendley presented his order form to the Johnsons as a basis for their agreement. If there is any ambiguity in it, it is fair to hold it against Pendley and construe it in favor of the Johnsons, because Pendley controlled the written terms of the agreement.

6. You can only recover once for one injury. The Johnsons could not recover the additional $300, because with the $1,200, they could get what they bargained for: a new floor.

A quick note about settlement: During settlement negotiations, Pendley offered to re-place the floor. The Johnsons declined because they didn't want Pendley to set foot in their house again. This is a common position taken by damaged parties. They may have been able to resolve it by agreeing on another installer to replace the floor and have Pendley pay for it, but they did not think about this possibility.

Pendley could have avoided the trial result by having the Johnsons sign a statement such as, "We know this new floor is made to go over the old one, and we give Pendley per-mission to glue it to the subfloor." This would have amounted to what in the construction industry is called a "change order." Pendley also could have done a better job.

For all consumers: A written change order should be completed whenever the job is changed by any service provider, mechanic, remodeler, plumber, or roofer. This is an exten-sion of The Paper Sack Rule: "If you have a contract and it changes, write the changes down on your paper sack."

The Case of "One Eye Is Private and the Other Doesn't See"

Sandra Whitney was sure that her brother Joseph was a bum and a drug abuser. But his wife was so sweet. So when Joseph's wife, Maria, sued him for divorce and for custody of four-year-old Quinton, Sandra decided to help. On the suggestion of Maria's lawyer, she hired private investigators John and Phyllis Adair to get the dirt on brother Joe. Private in-vestigators work on an hourly rate, plus expenses, so this was the basis of their agreement. Sandra eventually paid the Adairs more than $3,500 in fees for work over a two-month period.

The Adairs didn't find any dirt on Joseph (there wasn't any), and Sandra was mad. She wanted her money back. She sued for more than she paid the Adairs, because she felt the Adairs had misrepresented their ability to find nasty facts on Joseph. But the Adairs were prepared with arguments.

Their agreement was that Sandra would pay the Adairs for their time and effort in try-ing to get bad goods on Joseph. The Adairs emphasized early in their dealings with Sandra that it was impossible to guarantee the results of their investigation. They warned that there may not be anything to find, which turned out to be the case. Further, they explained that, unlike on TV or in the movies, their investigation techniques were limited because of right to privacy provisions in the law: They could not and would not illegally tap telephones, place hidden microphones or cameras in houses, or get records covered by doctor/patient confidentiality.

The Adairs did what they were supposed to do, there was no dirt to find, and ultimately, they won at trial.

Every contract for services is a contract for a person's time, attention, effort, and exper-tise. This is what every employer pays for, and this is all Sandra paid for. The Adairs agreed to investigate and report. They did and were entitled to their fees. In another context, the same result may flow from an auto mechanic's agreeing for a fee to take an engine entirely apart to see if he can find anything wrong with it. Finding nothing, he would still be entitled to his agreed-upon fee.

Variations of the same theme happen when a mechanic or attorney does preliminary work, but doesn't discover the extent or cost of fixing a problem "until he gets into it." We see more mechanic cases than lawyer cases in small claims court, with the plaintiff complaining that a $200 job ended up costing $1,200 because of what was found.

Usually the price and job are initially agreed upon, but when the mechanic gets in the engine, he discovers that further extensive work should be done to make the vehicle safe. The parties are at a crossroads: fix it, junk it, or pay for what has been done and fix the rest later. Communication breaks down, and everyone goes away angry and dissatisfied. The parties need to amend the contract, or enter another, but they are not willing to do it.

In "The Case of Fuschia Frustration," Sheila and Tom Waters hired interior decorator Terri Jones to do the paint, wallpaper, window treatments, and carpet in their new home. While Terri gave the Waters direction, the final specific decisions were left to the homeowners. Terri did all the work and then wanted to get paid. The Waters said, "*No. Sorry, we don't like the look. The fuschia curtains don't quite go with this gray rug.*"

But the judge said *yes* and awarded Terri her agreed-upon fee.

Except in the rare case that a worker expressly warrants that the customer will be completely satisfied, the degree of excellence will be enforced to the standard of "good workmanship."

The Case of "Chickens in the Sun Porch, Dogs in the Hall"

Poteet loved animals. He had been raised on a farm in the rural South and felt nostalgic for the days of his youth, surrounded by dogs, cats, chickens, and hogs.

On an oral lease, Marks rented Poteet a small two-story house in a rural area that was going suburban. It had two acres of land, lots of trees, and a full chain-link fence enclosing the back. The rent was $325 a month, with a $300 security deposit. Poteet paid his rent on time by sending it to Marks' home 25 miles away. Marks called once in a while to see if everything was going well, but stayed away from the property for the 18 months Poteet lived there. Marks trusted people and thought that all was well as long as he got the rent on time and he didn't get any midnight calls to fix the plumbing.

When the rent for the 19th month didn't come and the telephone recording reported that Poteet's telephone had been "temporarily disconnected," Marks went to investigate. He found a scene that resembled a very bad slasher movie.

As we say locally, this house was "tore up!" All the doors were scratched and chewed, just a few banister pickets remained, and all that was left of the wall-to-wall carpet were a few remnants stuck to the nail strips around the room edges.

Shockingly, the sun porch, a room 14 feet by 20 feet, was filled with chicken feathers and other chicken droppings, bloody parts, and debris. Feather trails and clumps were spread throughout the house.

The evidence at trial showed that not only did Poteet like chickens, but his two large dogs did, too. To them, the fowl were just fast food. Marks brought photos and his repairman to trial and won more than $4,500 in damages. Although you may think it was an open-and-shut case, but to the judge, it was a close decision.

Landlord and tenant relationships have existed for eons. Like other rules of law about relationships that have existed forever, basic residential landlord/tenant law is fairly uniform from state to state. On the other hand, when the landlord is in the business of renting many properties—when he is considered a "commercial landlord"—the law varies considerably from state to state. It depends upon the housing conditions particular to your state, be it primarily urban or rural, and the relative strength of the commercial real estate groups and tenant consumer groups in your state legislature.

In Marks's case, there was a question under local law as to whether his recovery was limited to the security deposit he took in the beginning of the lease. After all, it was given to secure damage to the property. Also, Poteet argued that much of the damage existed at the time he moved in, but the judge did not believe him. In any event, the rules that applied in this case made sense. Marks did not rent the property to Poteet so that Poteet's big dogs could teethe on the rugs and railings or fill it with chicken parts. Another variation of the First Rule of Commerce: You don't rent people your property so they can destroy it.

But Marks learned that it is unwise to be an absentee landlord—one who rents property, leaves, and stays absent. Many landlords who end up in court learn this rule the same hard way.

If you have questions about local law in this area, check your telephone directory for tenant help lines and real estate boards, or call the secretary of state to see what information is available. Your state bar association may also send out pamphlets or other information, and your local librarian may also help.

The Case of "The Vulcanized Check"

Well, not really "vulcanized." Those of you who are old enough might remember Vulcanization, a process that was advertised to make tire rubber last longer.

Rubber checks (bad checks) are a widespread and difficult problem in today's commercial world. Because merchants get so many worthless checks, and the numbers increase in bad economic times, most states have specific laws that make the writing of a bad check a semi-criminal or criminal offense. As a result, you may get additional damages if you sue in civil court—in some places, two or three times the face amount of the check—or you may have the bad check writer prosecuted criminally, without having to file a lawsuit yourself.

If you get a check returned from your bank stamped, "Insufficient Funds" or "Account Closed," call your local court clerk to find out what you can do to collect. You may be able to recover your money, your bank fees, and maybe more, without setting foot in the courthouse.

Now on to our case.

Bluffton was hearing "cranking, grinding, and mashing" noises in his 1978 Chevrolet pickup, so he took it to Rich to have the automatic transmission repaired. Rich listened to it and heard whirs, whines, and clanks. (Here's an example of people experiencing the same thing in different ways. This is how two witnesses can tell two stories about the same event without lying; they both believe they are right.) Rich wrote an Estimate/Work Order for Bluffton in the amount of $225 for the repair. Bluffton signed it and left.

Of course, when Rich started the job and "got into it," he found there was a lot more work to do than he originally thought. He tried, without success, to telephone Bluffton, and they played phone tag on their answering machines for almost a week. They never talked until after the work was done. Rich was at a crossroads: Further work may be unauthorized, but the car needed to be put back together. He fixed it. Bluffton would understand.

They met in Rich's garage and he gave Bluffton the bill for $525. Bluffton said what can politely be transcribed only as, "My Goodness! That certainly is much more than I thought it would be!" Eventually, he wrote a check for the repair and drove his truck off. The check bounced and ended up creating a negative balance in Rich's account when he tried to write checks relying on the deposit. Rich sued.

But what was the contract? Did Bluffton want it fixed, or only $225 worth of work done? Should he have to pay for work he didn't authorize? Did Rich take advantage of him?

The rich don't always win, but Rich won in this case. There, in the bottom left corner of the Work Order/Estimate, it read, "Estimates given prior to beginning work are just estimates. By signing this document, the customer authorizes the mechanic and his agents to perform all services that are deemed necessary to effect a repair with or without notice. All parts and labor are warranted for 30 days from the date of delivery."

Consumer tip: Many of the documents you sign for services make you subject to the conditions on the back. Read them.

The Case of "The No-account: Every Businessperson's Pet Peeve"

Unless you are a volunteer, if you work for someone, you expect to get paid. Most folks do get paid. Those who do not may find themselves in small claims court to collect.

Brookshire was a physical therapist, known widely in the community as being able to work wonders on patients everyone else considered hopeless. She employed an interdisciplinary approach: diet, water therapy, weight training, massage, and meditation. She liked her work, and was thrilled each time a patient made marked improvement.

Cole was deeply depressed. In the three years before she came to see Brookshire, she had seen countless doctors, traditional therapists, psychologists, chiropractors, and a hypnotist. At one time an avid cyclist, she had fallen while riding, injuring her right hip. She had no broken bones, but not long after, her leg grew weaker.

When she first saw Brookshire, Cole's leg had atrophied so much that she could only walk with a brace and a cane. A medical mystery, she had been referred to Brookshire by her neurologist. She was out of work and broke. She signed Brookshire's standard contract, and treatment began.

Brookshire applied her unique blend of treatments, and within three months, Cole could walk without the brace and cane. Within a year, she had fully recovered. Brookshire had expended $4,858 worth of effort on Cole's behalf, trusting that her patient would pay. Cole wouldn't pay. Brookshire sued.

Brookshire's standard contract said, "The patient understands that he/she is individually responsible for all fees, notwithstanding any insurance or co-insurance payments."

On trial night, Brookshire sent her bookkeeper, Trent, to court with the records of Cole's account.

Cole testified, "I never read the contract I signed; I couldn't pay her when she started and she knew it and I can't pay her now. I think she took advantage of me."

Brookshire got her judgment. Again the rules that applied made good common sense:

1. If you sign a contract and can read, and are not prevented from reading, you are bound by the contract.

2. If you promise to pay when you can't pay, and someone else does work relying on your promise, you must pay. If you accept work, even if you don't expressly promise to pay, the law will impose this promise on you.

3. Concerning Cole's argument that Brookshire had taken advantage of her: You cannot continue to accept valuable services knowing that you will not be able to pay for them.

4. Although Brookshire did not go to court herself, she sent someone who knew that Cole had received the services, and what was charged for them, and she had the regularly kept records of the business with her to back up her testimony.

The Case of "The Marriage That Never Was"

Mike and Debbie were in love, for a time. Two years before they ended up in my court, they moved in together, then bought the condo they lived in. Together, they furnished it: living room and bedroom furniture, microwave, patio furniture, an original oil painting for $300, and a small furry dog named Wolfred. (She wanted to name him Fred; he wanted to name him Wolf.)

After a while, small irritations grew and blossomed in the middle of their relationship. They grew apart. Then they moved apart. They came to court to partition the property they couldn't divide on their own: the patio furniture and Wolfred.

When they were accumulating things and memories, they never discussed the possibility of splitting up. Each assumed that if it happened, they would just divide things up "equally."

Mike argued that because Debbie had gotten more value in taking the living room furniture and the original art than he did in taking the bedroom furniture, it was only fair that he get the dog and the patio furniture. But Debbie loved the dog, too. She argued that it was mostly her money that paid for the deck furniture, and that she was the better "parent" to the dog.

This was a contract case with no contract, or only half a contract, which is the legal equivalent of none. They had agreed to share everything, with no thought of dividing it. They had differing notions of what was "equal" and "fair." All a judge could do was try to determine what was fair under all the circumstances.

The evidence showed that they had established a pattern of buying things: Each had more of an emotional attachment to a certain object, had the last word on buying it, and/or contributed more in paying for it. For example, Mike was attached to the CD changer. Debbie had paid more than half for the patio furniture, and she *was* the better parent.

The judgment was for Mike to be paid $175, conditioned on his return of the furniture and dog to Debbie. This was a kind of "forced sale" of Mike's interest in the furniture and dog. It was decided basically on fairness, but also on my constructing an agreement for them, based on how they acted toward the property.

Debbie didn't mind if Mike wanted to visit with the dog from time to time, but she neither asked for nor received "dog support."

The Case of "The Barter Gone Berserk"

Bill, owner of "Bill's Auto and Truck Repair," and Ron, owner of "Ron's Trucking," had a big idea: Bill would fix Ron's trucks, and Ron would fill in the large gully behind Bill's shop with fill dirt, so that Bill would have more parking and car storage.

They worked together for a year and a half. When the gully was full, Bill thought the contract was over. He figured it up, and gave Ron a $12,000 additional bill for car and truck repairs. They agreed on everything but the last $3,000, and Bill sued to recover the rest of his repair bill.

The evidence showed that Ron's drivers were bringing their own trucks to Bill's for service, as well as their business vehicles. Bill thought Ron knew. Ron didn't. Bill won. Ron did not pay attention to the performance of this contract and it got out of control. The court would not protect him against himself.

While they had agreed to perform services for each other, they had failed to agree on the value of their services and what vehicles were covered. They had no contract with each other while the performance was being undertaken by both of them for their mutual benefit. There had not been a "meeting of the minds" on all the necessary terms of the agreement. Bill was only able to win because he showed that the charges for the work he did were the same as what other mechanics in town charged for similar work. He was not a volunteer, so he was entitled to the reasonable value of his work.

Both felt foolish. Both vowed, "Never Again!"

The Case of "The Cagey Crooked Contractor"

Homeowner Winkler contracted with Bemis to rebuild his house. Bemis hired Bibb to redo the roof. Winkler paid Bemis, but Bemis did not pay Bibb and boogied to Bermuda. Bibb sued Winkler and won.

Despite the lack of a contract between Bibb and Winkler, Bibb falls into the previously mentioned category of people favored by the law. Because he had supplied labor and materials to improve Winkler's property, he had a right to recover his price from the property owner.

The law even gave him something extra: a *lien* on Winkler's house. A lien is a special charge on the property. Had Winkler not paid Bibb his judgment, Bibb could have had the sheriff of the county sell Winkler's house to satisfy the lien.

The moral for all Winkler's: Know who you are doing business with. (Note: We are *all* Winklers!)

The Case of "The Faded Angel"

When Abbot brought her dazzlingly white, but slightly soiled choir robe to Gillespie's Dry Cleaners before the big Easter show, she did not expect to have it come back gray.

Gillespie said, "I dry cleaned it twice. She told me to dry clean it."

Abbot testified, "It's ruined!" and brought another robe to court to compare it to hers and to show what it was supposed to look like. The second robe dazzled. It looked heavenly. Because Gillespie was the expert and should have known what process to use on the robe's fabric—or known enough not to touch it if he didn't—Abbot won. She rightfully relied on his expertise and was damaged.

Abbot's recovery in the case was limited to the fair market value of the robe that was damaged, not the replacement value she asked for. The robe was three years old. To award more than the actual value of the item at the time it was ruined would have given Abbot more than she lost.

The depreciation was easy to calculate in this case, because Abbot testified that the robes usually lasted 10 years with ordinary care. She won 70 percent of what she testified a new robe would cost.

The Case of "Is That Sewage I See Before My Eyes?"

One Sunday night, while Charlie and Alice Freeman were waiting to hear their microwave buzzer go off, Alice turned to Charlie and asked, "What is that horrible smell?"

They followed their noses to the hall outside their apartment and saw a brown puddle oozing toward them from the vacant apartment next door. Alice immediately got on the phone to the apartment complex management, while Charlie stuffed towels under their door to dam the flow. It almost worked.

For the next two days, the offensive liquid attacked and retreated in the hallway and under their door while the plumber tried to fix the problem.

The Freemans couldn't stay in their apartment because of the odor. Fortunately for them, they had friends to stay with during the three weeks it took to correct the problem. When they returned to their apartment, they found a three-foot brown stain on their plush front hall carpet, and they noticed a faint but distinct odor in the building, and on their furniture and clothes. The management could not get the stain out of their wall-to-wall carpet and refused to replace it. The smell never entirely went away. So, the Freeman's did.

The couple moved out with the consent of the landlord. Then they sued for the $650 rent they paid during the time they endured the odor and wetness and the time they lived with their friends.

They almost got it all. Like everyone who lives in property rented by a commercial landlord, they had a written lease prepared by the landlord that they signed when they moved in. It controlled their contractual relationship. Toward the end, in Paragraph 17, it stated, "For conditions beyond the control of Landlord rendering the premises untenantable, rent shall be abated in proportion to that portion rendered untenantable to the remainder of the premises." Because only about five percent of their floor was covered, under the lease, they could only recover five percent of the rent lost.

But the judge wasn't deterred. In other parts of the lease, it stated that the Landlord had the duty to make repairs when notified of a problem. The judge found that three weeks was beyond a reasonable time to make the repair. She awarded the Freemans all of their rent, except for two day's worth—the time of repair the judge found reasonable under the circumstances. The judge disregarded the strict lease law to do substantial justice in this case.

If the law had been strictly applied, the Freeman's would have recovered only $37.50, or five percent of the total they lost. The moral is: Read what you sign and know as much about the law as you can, but always argue what is reasonable and makes sense. You can determine what makes sense by weighing all the factors at work in your case, together with your notions of justice and fair play. It is highly likely that your position will parallel the legal principle that controls the outcome of your dispute.

CHAPTER 10

IS THE CASE CONTRACT, TORT, OR BOTH?

Human activities, like the people who are involved in them, don't always fit into neat categories. Likewise, there are some legal actions that mix elements of contracts and torts so thoroughly that you can't separate them. Torts are related in many ways to contracts. With contracts, a duty spelled out in an agreement may be violated, which results in injury. In the case of torts, the duty comes from general laws or customs. Cases involving a combination of contract and tort are different from pure torts only in the origin of the duty involved.

For example, in "The Case of the Provable Feast," Bailey went into his local hamburger outlet, Fare and Fast, and ordered their Big Bully Burger. He was into his third large bite when he bit into something hard and felt his teeth grind in a most uncomfortable way.

After he screamed, he looked to see what appeared to be a sprocket—a little steel wheel with teeth on the outside—sticking out of what was left of his Big Bully.

Bailey had to have expensive dental work done, and when Farr, the owner of Fare and Fast, refused to pay, Bailey sued in small claims court.

The case started with a contract: Bailey's promise to pay in exchange for Farr's promise to supply a burger to him. But there was also a general duty on the part of Farr to supply the food without anything being in it that was dangerous to her customer. This principle applies to any kind of goods sold new, not only food. So Bailey, who for a while was known as "Toothless Tony," could recover for the injury that resulted directly from Farr's failure to live up to her duty.

Small claims tort cases often begin with contracts. You lent your mini-chainsaw to your brother-in-law, Framus, so he could cut down some small alder trees. You didn't learn until too late that Framus, always looking for an angle, rented it to Frieda, his neighbor down the street, so she could cut down an old red oak tree.

If you got back what was left of your saw, you could sue Framus for damage to the saw because he *converted* it—used it inconsistently with your agreement. You could also recover the rent he got from Frieda, because Framus got it wrongfully.

The rule is, if you lend someone your property, and they use it in a way you did not foresee or give permission for, you may recover for this tort of *conversion.*

Conversion can be committed either intentionally or negligently.

In another example, you take your car in for a $60 repair, and when you get it back, your $75 tennis racket and $100 speakers are missing from the back. The repair shop committed "acts inconsistent with the limitations of their permitted possession and use of your property." This is a contract of *bailment,* where one person gives property to another, trusting that the one getting the property will take care of it while he or she is fixing it or improving it in some way. The conversion results from violating this trust.

Or you take your car in to the body shop to have a fender straightened, and when you get it back, your taillight is shattered. Again, the whole matter started with a contract—your promise to pay the shop owner for specific services. The duty that he breached was to not otherwise damage your property in the process.

Cases of *fraud and deceit* most often begin with a contract. Trickery in the marketplace is ancient and takes different forms as societies and technologies change. The ways people can commit fraud are so varied, even small claims courts, where everything is ordinarily informal, require that fraud claims be spelled out and proven very specifically.

The requirement of specificity protects anyone charged with fraud, because it is so easy to make a false claim of it and ruin a person's business reputation.

To win a fraud case, you need to prove all of these elements:

1. That the offending party made a false representation to you.

2. That at the time the false statement was made or deception done, the offender knew it was false. This means the falsehood was intentional, or at least made with a reckless disregard for the truth, not just negligence.

3. That at the time the misrepresentation was made, the offender intended that you rely on it.

4. That you did rely on it.

5. That you were damaged because you relied on it.

As you can see, this is by far the most legally technical type of case to prove in small claims court. But because scams are forever causing people misery, these claims often come up.

If you are accused of fraud and are defending against it, if there is no evidence to prove any *one* of the five elements listed, you should win.

While fraud usually involves the use of statements to deceive (for example, "This car has only 20,000 miles on it"), it can be committed by acts or even failures to act, such as failing to tell a customer any known defects about a car before a sale. For example, the car in question has been totaled twice and the front axle was taken from a 1946 Ford pickup and "doesn't fit quite right."

A claim of fraud cannot be based on statements about the future, because no one can see that far. And you cannot be deceived when you know that the representation made to you is false, or that it is too outrageous to be believed. It is unfortunate, but most fraud is perpetuated by playing on the victim's greed. The deceiver offers a deal that is just a little too good to be true. And it is. Again, the court will not be put in the position of protecting people from themselves. You simply need to be cautious in your business dealings.

The crux of fraud is intending to deceive and doing it successfully. Taking the defrauder to court gives you the chance to get even, and more. Because it is so nasty, you can get an additional award of damages called *punitive damages* (also called *exemplary* damages, to make an example of the offender) on top of those actual damages you can prove you lost because of the fraud. Punitive damages are awarded to prevent the wrongdoer from repeating the wrongful deeds or anything similar to them.

How much in punitive damages can you ask for or expect to receive? It is within the discretion of the judge to award them in the first place and to decide on the amount. This discretion will be exercised based on the circumstances of each case. Your best offense is to lay out all the facts and to be specific in describing all the ways the fraud has affected you. The top limit of the total damages you can win is the top limit of the court's jurisdiction.

In your Complaint, Statement of Claim, or Petition for Relief, you can ask for punitive damages in an amount, which, when added to the damages caused directly from the fraud, does not exceed the total amount your court has the power to award. If you think you deserve more, go to a different court to ask.

Those who have been cheated, or believe they have, often come to court with a big load of emotional baggage—they are very angry. If you are one of them, remember, it is just the facts and just the law that will propel you to victory. Settlement may still provide you with your best legal outcome.

You may find combinations of tort and contract cases in any of the following situations where the duties in a contract are not done, or are done improperly, and damage results:

1. A landlord has a general duty to keep the rented premises safe from known dangers. It's the same for shippers and truckers and their cargo.

2. Bus and cab drivers have a duty to transport their passengers safely and within the law.

3. Beverage bottlers and food packagers have a duty to keep foreign substances out of their products.

4. All people who supply services have a duty to perform them in such a way that other people and their property are not damaged. Painters, carpenters, repair people, plumbers, and exterminators cannot leave their tools lying around where kids can get at them. Veterinarians should not kill your pets while they are trying to cure them. Dry cleaners, auto mechanics, and the person in the fixit shop also have a duty to perform their jobs properly.

5. Manufacturers of all kinds, from the crafter at the weekend show to the multi-national conglomerate, have a duty to make their products safe to the consumer.

6. Businesses have a duty to their customers to keep their premises safe from known dangers. This is why you sometimes see "Caution: Slippery When Wet" signs around a store even when there is nothing wrong with the floor.

CHAPTER 11

High Crimes, Misdemeanors, and Ordinances

You can be the victim of a crime and still end up in small claims court to recover the damages suffered as a result of the offense against you.

A crime is the violation of a statute with criminal intent, criminal negligence or as part of a criminal scheme or undertaking. The type of statutes known as "criminal" statutes are those that are meant to prohibit or prevent conduct that unjustifiably causes harm to a citizen, simply because he is a citizen, a member of the public. Crimes are offenses against society as a whole, although they may affect only one citizen at a time.

These statutes are made into law by the legislatures of the different governmental units. City and county statutes are known as ordinances. In order to meet the tests of your state and the federal constitutions, they are written so that they give fair warning to all of the prohibited conduct.

The same kind of personal injury damage or property damage you can suffer as the result of a tort can be the result of a crime. White collar crimes usually involve injuries to business interests, and often involve fraudulent conduct.

If you are the victim of a crime, the rights that are violated are said to be public rights, because a crime is an offense against the general peace and dignity of all persons. As a victim, technically you are only a witness in a criminal case, like any other witness. The prosecutor represents all the people and works for the government. She is the lawyer on your side because you are a member of the society whose laws she has sworn to enforce, but the attorney-client relationship, one derived from a private contract, does not exist between you.

A person convicted of a crime is punished. Incidental to the punishment, the wrongdoer may also be ordered to pay *restitution*. When restitution is ordered as part of a sentence, the convicted person is ordered to restore to the victim the provable value of the damage resulting from the crime. Most of the time this payment is a condition of the guilty person's staying out of jail. As a result, there is a greater likelihood of your being made whole financially when restitution is ordered as part of the sentence in a criminal case, and when it is made a condition of the criminal remaining free. In this case, the criminal defendant holds the keys to the jailhouse in his hand and does not need to go there at all unless you are not paid. People will quickly come up with money with the threat of a lockup hanging over their heads. Unless the criminal has a long record, it is likely that you will be paid without having to file a lawsuit.

If you have suffered damage as the result of the crime, you need to be able to show the prosecutor the dollar value of the damage and to let the prosecutor know that you would like to be notified at every stage of the case. Be persistent. If you have not been notified about the progress of the case for a time that seems long to you, call the prosecutor. After all, he or she works for you, the taxpayer.

If you can, go to the sentencing hearing, let the judge know you are the victim, and tell him or her how much you have lost. You may get it back. But being the victim of a crime does not do away with your rights to bring a civil action for the damage done to you. If restitution is not ordered as part of the sentence in the case, or even if the bad guy is found not guilty at trial, you keep your right to sue and recover, just as in any other case where you have suffered a substantial loss. A defendant in a criminal case must be proven guilty of the crime to a moral certainty and beyond a reasonable doubt—a very difficult level of proof. This is why a criminal defendant is never found *innocent*, only *not guilty*, if acquitted. To win in a civil case, you need only prove that your evidence is a little better than that offered by the opposition. It needs to weigh a little more on the scales of justice. Simply because a prosecutor fails to prove an act beyond a reasonable doubt does not mean that you cannot prove it by the greater weight of the evidence.

One special caution in these cases: Statistics show that 90 percent of crimes are committed by 10 percent of the population. Statistics show, too, that most of that 10 percent is not going to have money or property to satisfy your claim even if you get judgment against them. If they have nothing, you may end up with nothing but the warm feeling that comes from having met the challenge of doing something you have not done before.

If you want to pursue your claim as a matter of principle, because you are in a business where it is likely you will need to learn how to win a small claims case, or because you think it would be fun, go ahead! The person who has no money now might have some later. Judgments stay alive, and are collectible for extended periods—up to seven years in many states.

PART III

LET THE WAR GAME BEGIN

Chapter 12

Getting Free (or Nearly Free) Good Legal Advice

I'm not fooling. Legal advice that is good can also be free, or nearly free. If, after you have analyzed your case as much as you can, you have more questions than answers, do the logical thing: Ask someone who should know.

First, disregard the conventional wisdom, "There is no such thing as a free lunch" and "You get what you pay for." Who said so, anyway? The best things in life are still free. Just because an item costs more, it does not mean that it is better; nor if it costs less, that it is faulty.

For many reasons, competent lawyers will talk to you for no pay. I will let you know later how to find an attorney. For now, you should know *why* a lawyer will be glad to talk to you, and what you should ask.

Attorneys have notoriously big egos. No one is sure if this profession attracts people who think a lot of themselves, or if lawyers just grow their overlarge egos once they are in the profession. I think that to a great extent, lawyers' inflated opinions of themselves are emotional armor against empathy for their clients' pain. In any event, by seeking their advice, you are flattering them for their accomplishments. You implicitly recognize that they are experts in a special field of knowledge.

As a result, when you ask a lawyer a legal question, he or she will experience an overwhelming urge to give you an answer. A pride in being right goes along with the ego. The answer you get will be the lawyer's best answer based on the situation as you have related it.

Which brings us to an important point: Your answers will only be as good as your questions. You need to be certain to relate *all* the important facts in your case in a logical way, including those that you know or suspect may be favorable to the other side in your dispute. This takes planning. Write your questions out, or at least outline all the points you want to touch on with the lawyer. You should be succinct. An attorney will be initially eager to grace you with a free opinion. But that enthusiasm fades quickly, and is replaced by suspicion that what you are really looking for is free legal advice.

If your questions are brief and complete, your answers are likely to be right for another reason: Attorneys who are in business flourish or fail based on their reputations. They want to earn a reputation for being right, honest, and fair. Wrong advice can seriously damage a good reputation. If people get bad advice, other people will find out about it. If it turns out that the opinion given to you is wrong, it is probably because the attorney did not know all the pertinent facts about your case, or simply the result of a mistake, rather than an intentional attempt to mislead you.

Finally, a lawyer's free advice is likely to be correct because, at least at first, he or she will think there is a fee in it. Don't report the dollar amount you are seeking until the last part of your conversation. If an attorney learns that your dispute involves a minimal dollar amount, it is likely your conversation will end quickly.

Any time you talk to an attorney, carefully weigh the advice you get. Decide if it makes sense. If you have any anxiety about the value of the first opinion, go get another one. No matter whom you encounter that you suspect may have more information than you do about the civil justice system, there is one rule you should always remember: There's no harm in asking.

Where do you go? Before you seek out a lawyer for advice, call the clerk of your local small claims court (see Appendix 1 on page 161). Clerks who have worked in the courts for a while have a wealth of practical knowledge about how cases are treated in their courts. They are prohibited from giving out legal advice, but they do it anyway. Part of what clerks can explain is how to get your case through their particular court. In the process, they will give you general advice based on their having seen hundreds of cases like yours go through the system. There is no harm in asking, but be sure and keep your questions brief and clear.

You can say something like, "My case involves (give a summary of your case). Is this the kind of case that is handled by your court?" Avoid asking, "Do you think I'll win?" The more detail you are able to relate in your conversation with the clerk, the more likely you are to receive useful clues.

Court clerks tend to be very busy. It's best to call early in the day for best results. If you are having an easy conversation with a clerk, you can also ask, "If I decide I need a lawyer to help me in this case, can you give me the names of some that regularly do a good job in your court?" It may be that the clerk is prohibited from recommending any one lawyer, but it may be acceptable to give you several to choose from.

Call your local bar associations. There is one in each county, in each large city, and certainly one in each state. If there is more than one in your telephone book, call them all. Many have services that provide a brief consultation with one of the association members for a minimal fee, usually between $25 and $50 for a fixed amount of the attorney's time, ordinarily 30 minutes. You are not financially obligated to the attorney or bar association after that time unless you reach an agreement with the lawyer about it. When you have analyzed your case and think you have a winner, or are not quite sure, or you face the loss of hundreds of dollars if your analysis is wrong, you may want to make this small investment.

There are also private, for-profit lawyer referral services listed in your yellow pages. Their costs and terms vary. The call is free. Our local telephone company has a free call-in line providing general legal advice on a recording. These phone ads are sponsored by attorneys who will have a short blurb during the ad about their areas of practice.

If you look in the telephone book, you may find lawyers who advertise free initial consultations. You can have as many of these as you can stand!

Do you know a lawyer socially? People are forever coming up to me and asking to discuss their current legal problem. Usually, I answer their questions because it's the polite thing to do, and I give the best answer that I can. (The truth: I look at my watch for a long time to let them know I get paid for giving legal advice. Then I answer.) You might not get all the information you need in this informal way, but you will still get information of value.

If you have a law school in your community, see if it has a student clinic or "hotline" to field legal questions. What law students do not have in experience, they make up for in enthusiasm. The best answer you can get from a law student is, "Let me do some research and get back with you on it." Find out when you can expect to hear back. They will do the work, but make sure you follow up.

Another good source of information is your local legal radio talk show. Most radio stations employ attorneys who know what they are talking about. From time to time, stations have off-the air call-in opportunities. Call in. There is no harm in asking.

You can call an attorney with the most tenuous contact. If you know nothing else about the lawyer than his name and that he is a "great guy" because you got his name from a friend of a friend, let the lawyer know. Attorneys love referrals, no matter what the source.

If all else fails, cold call a lawyer. Look in the yellow pages for attorneys advertising specialties in the area of law involved in your case. It is more likely you will be able to talk for free to a lawyer who works alone or in a very small firm. Say, "I have a problem and I need to ask a few questions before I decide if I need to hire a lawyer. Can you help me?" Know what you will say after he says, "Of course."

You may end up talking with the attorney's paralegal. These are legal paraprofessionals having a general law background, and a working understanding of how the legal system runs. If they are experienced, they also will have a thorough working knowledge of the areas of law of their bosses' specialties. Some are very careful to avoid giving legal advice, but they do, just as clerks do.

You can even get second and third opinions this way. This process is cheap and fairly reliable. Again, most attorneys know that they strive forward or fall back on the value of their reputations. Again, the only danger is tht the value of what you get from this exchange is only as good as what you put in.

If you visit an attorney, be prepared. If you know you will have to pay for the attorney's time, no matter how short, get the most for your money. Before you talk to any attorney, face to face or on the phone, summarize your case in writing in 100 words or less. This will serve two purposes: 1) It will give you a useful handle on your case and provide an overview you can use later should you need to summarize your case for a judge; and 2) Once the attorney knows the crux of your case, he or she will ask you questions to find out what the lawyer thinks is important to the outcome. Most lawyers have busy, curious minds. They will want to know more about your case and will give you more information than you pay for if you let them.

On the same sheet of paper as your summary, list the questions you need answered. The first should be, "What do I need to know about my case to win?"

This question is for you. The specific questions that you list in response are for the attorney. This meeting involves your time and money; it only involves the attorney's time. If the attorney rambles off the subject, bring him or her back! You can make friends with the lawyer once you know all you need to know about the case.

If your case is an easy winner, and a valuable one, the attorney may ask if you want legal representation. Say that you will call back. And always be sure to ask how much it will cost for the lawyer to represent you.

Good hunting.

CHAPTER 13

SETTLEMENT: WINNING WITHOUT FIGHTING

You have verified that you have a claim that a court will hear and you think you might file a lawsuit. Or maybe you have received a demand from someone saying they have a claim against you that is headed for court. What next?

First, let's assume that you are a potential plaintiff. You have a claim or several claims against someone else and you know how much you will sue for. Here's a simple solution: Ask them for it. You may just resolve this thing without going any further. There's no harm in asking. The advantage is obvious: You may get the matter settled without further time and effort.

Asking for what is owed you can take many forms. Some people have a talent for writing demand letters with increasing degrees of seriousness. It is a simple matter to put your demand in writing. Deciding exactly what to write will help you be clear about what you want in order to resolve your dispute. Your demand letter can also guide you in defining the issues that may result in a trial if you need to sue.

What if you are the defendant? If you have received a complaint letter and you want to know what the complainer will take to get off your back, the same principle applies: Ask. If you get a demand in writing, send your response the same way. But be sure that you respond. Court cases are often the results of broken communication.

Settlement and settlement negotiations make up the middle part of the civil justice process. Ninety percent of all cases filed by attorneys are settled without trial. This is because attorneys know that their clients most often gain their best legal advantage through settlement. They know, too, that this is all any attorney can do for a client: Make their client's best legal advantage tangible. Investigating the facts and researching the applicable law with a pinch of legal experience are the means to gain the best legal outcome. And lawyers get paid very well for doing it.

If the principle of the matter in your dispute is not so great, or your ardor has faded after the initial shock of the wrong done to you, or if you take pride in your intelligence, a full investigation of settlement prospects is for you.

The law loves settlement and compromise. It is the only realistic way to unclog the logjam caused by too many cases and not enough courtrooms, personnel, or time. Small claims courts are particularly in a crunch with the increasing number of cases they are required to hear. While they want to make a court accessible to those who have valid claims that they cannot reconcile on their own, the courts simply cannot handle the volume.

So, take a moment or two for a little soul searching. Even though by now you may have realized that you want to go for it—you want your trial—you should still weigh all the advantages and disadvantages of that decision against the certainty of gaining a favorable final disposition of your claim through settlement. Whether you are the person suing or the person sued, the same principles apply. Although the defendant in any lawsuit has the advantage of not having to prove anything and may also just want a day in court, you should have at least one eye open to conciliating your case.

From now all the way to the moment before the judge announces a final decision in open court at the end of your trial, there are many reasons to seriously consider settlement. The following list is not exhaustive:

- ◆ **The rules of your local court may require it.** In many states and cities, the legislators that have created your courts and court rules may love settlement so much that you are required to at least try to settle your case. This means that you actually do communicate with the other side about resolving your dispute. Talk to them. You may need to let the other side see all of your exhibits and even interview your witnesses. Check with the clerk about this before you file a suit.

- ◆ **You are more likely to get what you came for.** History has shown that when disputing people settle a matter and one of them is going to pay money to the other as the result, the person who is to get paid is more likely to get the money. The payer is more likely to pay if he or she is free from the fear of having to pay more and from the fear of having unsavory things happen to him or her, such as seizure of a car, freezing a bank account, or seizure of wages through garnishment. All of these can result from having a judgment against him or her. (See Chapter 23 for more on this.)

As a plaintiff, when you win, what you get is a judgment. This is a piece of paper that says you now have the right to go out and try to collect enough of the loser's cash or other property so you can get paid. Again, if the loser has no cash or property or no promise of any, all you will end up with is your piece of paper. If you know that there is a real likelihood that the defendant has little, you may consider getting what you can and reducing your losses. Your judgment could also drive the loser into bankruptcy. If you know that the defendant has been sued many times and lost, this may be a real possibility. If he or she bankrupts, you will likely get little or nothing.

The likelihood that you will recover all of your loss goes up when there is insurance covering it. Personal or property damage done in a home or business may be covered by homeowner's or business liability insurance. It is to the wrongdoer's advantage to tell you about insurance coverage because he or she has already paid the premium to cover your loss. If there is insurance, you will be negotiating with the insurance company's adjuster, or if a suit has been filed, with the company's attorney. The company's representative may ask you to supply them with specific information on a pre-printed form or in some other way. The small inconvenience of doing it their way far outweighs the risk of not recovering if you need to litigate your claim to the end. Play their paper game, but be sure you read and understand everything you are asked to sign. Make and keep a copy for your records.

♦ **You will feel better.** This is not an insignificant or silly reason. When you submit your dispute to a third person for a decision, you lose control of it. There is a psychological principle at work here. In our society, where mature, thinking individuals ought to be able to go through life resolving their problems without outside interference, we believe that if we must give up a problem to someone else, we have failed. This is not true, but the perception is there, nevertheless. If you settle, you control the outcome, and to whatever extent it is significant, you will have maintained control over that part of your life that is represented by this particular challenge.

♦ **Justice is nearly blind.** Only you and your witnesses know what really happened a month, two months, or six months before your trial. Memories always fade and get muddled, more so when the events are complicated. There is a legal legend about the car crash at an intersection. Witnesses on each of the four corners tell a completely different version of the incident at the scene of the accident, and each has a strangely different version from even his or her own original story when it is related at the trial. By comparing them, someone hearing them could not even be sure the information was about the same event.

Even if your witnesses remember every detail, there is no way that a judge can know all that really happened based on 15 to 30 minutes of testimony, and a quick look at all of your other evidence. At best, the verdict will be based on a mere thumbnail sketch of the whole story. Part of what judges do in making decisions is to decide whom to believe. The judge is a stranger to you and your controversy. He or she is just as likely at the outset to believe your opponent as to believe you. The judge may choose to believe the other party's witnesses or give greater weight to their documents and photographs. He or she may disregard or discount what you feel is the strongest part of your case, and give great credit to your adversary's version of things.

It does not matter so much that your cause is right and true; the important thing is how it will be *perceived*. This raises a serious question about justice. In support of this concept, tell the truth, the whole truth, and nothing but the truth. There is some weakness in every claim. If you tell your story with its flaws exposed, the judge is much more likely to believe it.

◆ **Judges are human.** Being a judge, I know that deep down inside, every one of us has a heart of gold. It may just take considerable digging to reach it. Because judges are human, they may, from time to time, make a mistake in judgment. There is no magical mathematical or other fixed formula for making a decision in your case that is "correct" in some universal sense. So—and attorneys will tell you this—there is always some unpredictability in submitting a case to a judge or a jury at trial.

There are other intangibles to consider. I have not done any research on this, but I am suspicious that even the best judges may unconsciously favor certain kinds of people over others. For example, unusually attractive people, widows, orphans, and little old ladies tend to be favored over unusually unattractive or hard-edged, brassy people, used car salesmen, and drug dealers. Nasty people probably lose more than nice people. As I say, this hunch is just a hunch, based totally upon speculation.

When I was leaving my law office one day on the way to the courthouse to preside in small claims court, there was a man sitting in the reception area waiting for another lawyer in my office. When I told the receptionist that I was headed over to court, the man offered, "Good luck—you never know what those crazy judges and juries are going to do." He's got the idea!

◆ **Try as everyone may, the playing field may not be level.** Though the civil justice system is based on an underlying principle of equality, some classes of citizens are favored in the law. It may be from the nature of their work, the power of their lobby in the legislature, or simply a matter of public policy that a group is favored.

You recall that some classes of workers have a right to a special claim on your property, a lien. Auto mechanics and other persons who repair and otherwise add value to their customers' property often have the right to keep the property until they are paid. This is a *possessory lien*. This is true even when the bill is contested. Similarly, plumbers, painters, roofers, and other construction trades may have a right to place a *mechanic's* or *materialman's lien*, a public notice of claim on your real estate to secure payment for work on your house, even where the quality or value of the job done is disputed.

Banks, insurance companies, and doctors are favored owing to their political clout. Preferences for them are written into the law. Banks are protected by provisions of the Uniform Commercial Code, which is adopted in most states. Ordinarily, there are technical legal hoops you must jump through before you can sue a doctor or other professionals for malpractice.

By greater experience in business or the law, the other party in your dispute may have placed themselves in a superior position in their contract with you. It is in the fine print. You may have pledged your furniture, appliances, and even your family dog as collateral on a loan, and may be legally helpless if they are repossessed. Landlords or tenants may have an advantage based on the strength of their lobbies and the extent to which your state is urbanized.

Is your potential opponent a member of a favored class in your state? Are you?

♦ **There may be more pain than gain.** You may recall the story of Ahearn and Hartley in Chapter 8, who lost a 30-year friendship over $100 and a worn-out lawn tractor. If your claim is against a long-time friend, business associate, or relative, nothing will more quickly destroy the relationship than the prosecution of a lawsuit. Whether you are the plaintiff or the defendant in a legal dispute, you have an emotional investment in its outcome. Plaintiffs universally want to be made whole. Defendants want their reputations restored after having been sued on what they may consider a frivolous complaint. To some extent, both feel victimized.

As your case gets closer to trial, your emotional investment will either grow or shrink. The smaller it gets, the more rational your decisions concerning settlement will become. If it grows, or is recognizably monstrous already, you should weigh the potential winning of the case at trial against the damage it could do to your relationship with the other party. In my court, I have seen brother against brother, and daughter against mother. Though a decision was rendered in each case, nobody won.

If the emotional investment in your case grows, it may also interfere with the rational preparation and presentation of your case at trial. To the extent that you are immobilized by anger, frustration, or any strong emotion, you will be a less effective litigator. High emotions can interfere with your getting the best legal outcome. In one case, the plaintiff was so angry that after he had called the defendant as a witness and grilled her for 15 minutes, he called no other witnesses and forgot to prove any part of his case.

♦ **The human factors may not be in your favor.** Look at yourself. Look at your opposition. Look at everyone who is likely to testify in your case. When you relate your version of the facts at trial, and when your witnesses do the same, will they be convincing? This may be only a minor concern. Most people are good storytellers when the story is true. But the very young or very old witness may become flustered. Non-English speaking or inarticulate witnesses simply may not be understood, thus their testimony may discounted.

All you have seen and heard about civil trials may fill you with fear about testifying under oath in a courtroom before a person wearing a black robe. This may be true even though your fear has been diminished by your careful preparation and all the knowledge gained by reading this book. Consider settlement as a real possibility at any point in the process that you realize you may not be able to win.

While I firmly believe that any citizen in ordinary circumstances has the wherewithal to successfully prepare and try a case in a small claims court, it may simply not be for you. If you decide it is not, don't give up! And don't sell your soul to reach a settlement at any cost. Your goal remains to reach a resolution of your dispute to your best advantage under all the circumstances. Your personality is just one factor. If you don't want to work out the settlement details, you can always hire a lawyer to worry and to work them out for you.

♦ **Your time is worth something.** It is worth a lot! Our time, whatever it is, is all we have. It is a nonrenewable resource. Preparing your case for trial and presenting it at trial is challenging and educational. Once done, it's fun. But when you evaluate your case and look at the time and effort it will take to investigate, prepare, and try your case, and also consider the value of your time, you may be better off going fishing, joining a community chorus, rebuilding that '49 Ford pickup in your garage, volunteering, or spending a couple of hours with your family or at work.

The prospect of a reasonable settlement may be more valuable if your investment of time, attention and effort is greater than the value of the return it will provide.

If you are a defendant, you may want to consider a settlement to avoid the time and effort necessary to defend even a groundless claim. Giving this advice flies in the face of all I believe about individual responsibility and the necessity to fight injustice wherever you find it; nevertheless, it is still sound advice.

You could win! What you win is a judgment, a piece of paper that says you now can start the collection process. Usually, the court will not collect your judgment for you. Often, the time and effort involved in the collection process is as much or more as the amount of time taken up by preparation and trial.

♦ **You could lose.** Your dispute may have started because you made an avoidable mistake, one you would not have made if you had been reasonably diligent. Courts will not protect you from yourself. If you are the author of your own misery, you will be responsible for reaching the conclusion of your story.

There can be only one winner. Even though you are convinced that you have the perfect case, open and shut, there is always a possibility, no matter how remote, that you could lose. I have seen lawyers come out of courtrooms shaking their heads, with looks of disbelief on their faces after getting totally unexpected negative results in "sure-win" cases.

Remember, in order to win, your total evidence must be stronger than that of your opposition. For plaintiffs or defendants asserting a counterclaim, you have a burden to prove your case by the greater weight of the evidence. It needs to be only *slightly* greater, but greater nonetheless. The scales of justice need to be tilted at least slightly in your favor.

After you know all you can reasonably know about your case, witnesses, and exhibits, and you know all you can about the case for the other side—its weaknesses and especially its strengths—you should be fairly certain you will win. This gives credit to all the uncertainties of trying a case and submitting it to a judge or jury for consideration. Your certainty level can be lower when your case is being pursued mainly on a matter of principle. If you have a valid, substantial, and provable claim and cannot reach a satisfactory agreement with the other side to resolve it, head for the courthouse. That is why it was built.

Negotiation tactics are covered in the next chapter. If you do reach an agreement, put it in writing. There are forms in the back of this book to help. If your small claims suit has already been filed, you should submit your agreement to the judge for approval. At least notify the clerk that your case has been settled, and ask what you should do next.

CHAPTER 14

NEGOTIATING YOUR SETTLEMENT

I hope you agree that exploring the possibility of settlement in your case will be worthwhile. The overall goal is to get the best settlement possible under the circumstances.

There are two popular approaches to negotiating settlements: *haggling* and *interest-based*. For each, you need to know all the facts and law you can, positive and negative. And you should take the moral and ethical high road—that is, within the boundaries of the negotiation approach you take, be forthright, honest, and up-front. Avoid emotion. You are not negotiating world peace, and it is not your life or your soul, nor those of your loved ones, that is at stake. It is only money, something money can buy, or an emotional investment you are compromising. Keep it in perspective.

Haggling

This approach, also known as the *positional approach*, to reaching a compromise is as old as commerce itself, and it is the one we are most familiar with. Many of us learned it early when negotiating how many potato chips we could have or bargaining a curfew with our parents. It is still practiced widely throughout the world, from Middle East open-air markets to the flea markets on Route 41 in Georgia. The goal in the game is to reach a middle ground both parties can live with. In the final outcome, each side wants the best part of that middle.

At the start of this approach to reaching a settlement, each party has an entrenched position, knows what won't be acceptable, and has at least a vague sense of what the absolute minimum needed to end the negotiating and settle the dispute will be. The idea is to come as close to the ideal solution, and thus, give up as little as possible.

Through a series of offers, refusals, and counteroffers, each party whittles away at the other party's position until the middle ground is reached. Despite my caution above to be honest and forthright, this approach requires some deception. If you let the other side know immediately what your bottom line is, the other side may accept, but you will always suspect you could have gotten more. So withhold that information until its strategic importance is maximized. Save your best bargaining chip for last.

The process allows for some inventiveness, if you can think of possible alternate solutions to your dispute as you exchange offers and counteroffers. The process ends when you agree or agree that you cannot agree.

The tactics usually take these or similar forms:

♦ Let the other side know of your willingness to negotiate, that you are willing to talk with them seriously about settling your case. Your first offer will be one that is very favorable to you. To make it effective, you should frame it so that there is just a very slight chance that the other side will accept it. If you keep some reality in it, the other side will not be offended, think your offer is ridiculous, or that your willingness to settle is just a ruse.

It may be safer to let the other side make the opening offer. This will give you a gauge on their position, and it may very well be more than your bottom line. You could end this in the first round!

♦ Keep making counteroffers until you settle or agree that you cannot reach a compromise. Don't be in a hurry. By asking the other side why they think their position is reasonable, or by asking other questions about their position, you do two things: 1) You can make a more informed decision about what your final position will be, and 2) You will learn a lot about the other side's case if you cannot settle, and you need to have a trial.

Knowing that you have taken my earlier advice and have kept your negotiations rational, businesslike, and free of emotion, if you do not settle, leave the door open for future discussions after each of you have had time to digest everything involved in your first settlement session. Avoid take-it-or-leave-it positions, insults, and threats. Remember, there are many good reasons why 90 percent of the civil cases handled by lawyers are settled prior to trial. And many are settled "on the courthouse steps" just before trial is about to begin. Keep your options open.

The Interest-based Approach

This approach is geared to meet the legitimate interests of the parties, instead of mechanically splitting the differences between positions. The advantage is that you are more likely to settle, and it is more likely that your compromise will be satisfactory, even rewarding, to both of you.

But this approach assumes a lot. It assumes that both parties agree that a settlement will result, that both will do what is necessary to reach that end, and that both will come to the bargaining table with the attitude, "Now what can we do to settle this thing?"

Your viewpoint on your legal claims is different here. Instead of concentrating on your position in the matter and what your bottom line is, you try to identify, then fulfill, your interests in the case. It takes some analysis. Answering the following questions can help with that analysis: What do your really want? Revenge? An apology? To be restored to the place you were before you started dealing with the other party? Is it just dollars and cents? What interests have been affected by the transactions that make up your complaint against the other party—your sense of security in your person or possessions? Your sense of the way things should be ordered in your world? Your sense of honesty or integrity? Your sense of having been betrayed or abandoned by someone you trusted?

The point of this process is for each party to understand what is really important in their case, beyond the dollars and cents. Once you know what is important, the tactics are simple: *You talk to the other side and listen to what they have to say, and then talk to them some more.* It is often true that the whole case may be caused by lack of communication. A dispute can continue for the same reason. Here are some points to keep in mind:

♦ The real difference between you and the other side concerning your dispute is the difference in the way you think about it. Find out what they think and why. Put yourself in their shoes.

♦ Remove blame from the mixture. Without the two of you, there would be no dispute. In hindsight, you should be able to see where you contributed to the creation or perpetuation of the conflict.

♦ Don't avoid your emotions about the dispute, recognize them in each other, and deal with them like any other fact making up your disagreement.

♦ When you recognize what values have been affected by the transactions that make up your dispute, you can make proposals consistent with your findings. You can be inventive. Unlike the positional approach, you can be honest. You may find that your interests can best be met by forgetting about your dispute and walking away from it.

If you reach an accord, you may find that the outcome is something you could not have imagined when you began the process. To those who have not been involved in negotiating this way, the outcome may even seem disagreeable or foolish. But if it best meets the legitimate interests you have identified, you have won, no matter how your settlement looks on paper. It may be ironic, but you can know that you have won, that you have met your needs, while the rest of the world believes you lost. If your real needs are met, you have won in the deepest sense.

As you can see, this approach takes a great degree of trust in yourself, in the other party, and in this process. The more you have at stake, the more worthwhile accepting the challenge of undertaking this process will be.

Knowing both ways in which you can negotiate settlements, you may find yourself borrowing from each system to meet the needs of your personality, that of the other side, or the peculiarities of your case. These approaches and the pros and cons of each are more fully set out and well explained in Roger Fisher and William Ury's book, *Getting to Yes* (2nd edition, Viking Penguin, 1991).

The first step is recognizing that settlement is an honorable and beneficial way to end your dispute. You can use any reasonable means to that end. There may be structures in place to help you along. Owing to the increase in lawsuits, and pressure on local governments to reduce spending on courts and staff, "Alternate Dispute Resolution" is a hot phrase in the legal community today. Various forms of mediation, arbitration, and mini-trials exist to increase efficiency in the courts and to reduce costs. These alternate forms are mandatory in some courts, so you will need to check to see what prevails in your court. The following is a summary of the forms of dispute resolution.

Mediation is the most common form. A mediator is a neutral third person who facilitates settlement discussions. The mediator usually has no authority to decide the dispute or to force a settlement.

Arbitration involves your presenting a summary of your case and arguing it to a neutral third person who makes a decision, which may be either binding or nonbinding. If binding, there is usually an appeal back to the regular court for a full trial. Arbitration is very much like a small claims trial, and you have a chance to test your case before it finally matters. Incidentally, both parties may be satisfied with the outcome.

In small claims courts where jury trials are available, *mini-trials* or *mock jury trials* may be available, too. As in arbitration, the case is presented in an abbreviated form, but before a panel of disinterested persons who render a decision. A judge, magistrate, or commissioner will preside to assure that the law is understood and the local rules of procedure followed. Again, ordinarily the case may be appealed for a full judge or jury trial.

These alternative forms of dispute resolution work particularly well in small claims cases where the amount in controversy is not so great, and where one or both parties' interests may simply be having their day in court. One of these forms can help you resolve your dispute more quickly than you would in a court trial.

CHAPTER 15

WHEN SHOULD YOU HIRE A LAWYER?

Hire a lawyer? Yes. I don't dislike nor distrust lawyers. After all, I am one. Despite critical references in other places in this book, practicing law is an honorable profession, mostly undertaken by people who are diligent and honest. I simply believe that they do not belong in small claims court, with the exception of some unusual cases.

The legal profession has taken a lot of bad press over recent years. Negative comments and constant bad humor pop up in the media with regularity. I heard my current favorite second-hand. A friend told me she saw a stand-up comedian who swaggered out on stage, with a big smile and big cowboy boots, and introduced his act, "Like my new boots? They're lawyer skin!"

Despite the efforts of local, state, and national bar associations to instill and enforce high ethical standards, we constantly hear about corrupt lawyers. It makes for good press, but it is an inaccurate depiction of the profession as a whole. As in every definable group, there are a few bad oysters that spoil the chowder.

The overwhelming majority of attorneys work hard to gain the best legal advantage for their clients. Trial lawyers have big egos by necessity. As advocates, they must wholeheartedly adopt and urge their clients' causes even in the face of contrary facts, law, and staunch opposition. To them, winning may not be everything, but it's high on the priority scale.

Lawyers who demand and receive large fees do so because they are worth it to their clients. They would not be worth it if they were not consistently good at what they do. As noted above, lawyers' careers flourish or falter on the strength of their reputations, built one client at a time.

Students are attracted to law for many reasons, but the hope of making a lot of money is usually not the most significant. Law presents the challenge to learn as much as you can about an ever-changing body of knowledge. One can never know all there is to know, because the law always changes. It has breadth covering all facets of ongoing human endeavor, and the depth of thousands of years of history. Some people who decide to pursue a legal career look at the law as a means of helping people in a meaningful way. Others want their lives to have impact on society. Most believe they can make a positive difference in the world.

The law is as old as humanity. Its current concepts and the language used to express them are nearly as old. Like other professions, it has its own jargon, obscure to those who are not trained in the law.

People fear, dislike, and distrust lawyers because they can't understand them. As stated earlier, some people believe that the obscurity of legal lingo gives lawyers a key to some mysterious treasure chest of knowledge that, when applied to their legal problem, will yield miraculous results. There is not one key, but many. There is information provided here and in other sources you may go to learn about the workings of the law: other books, seminars, "People's Law Schools," law courses offered by your local college's continuing education department, newspaper and magazine articles on law related subjects, and of course, the Internet. There is no mystery in the law, but it has a mystique that constantly draws our interest no matter what our situation in life, as is apparent by the enduring popularity of law related television shows, movies, and novels.

There are a lot of lawyers in this country, but you can briefly count the few who have earned reputations by pursuing frivolous suits. The weight of media hype in the rotten lawyer cases will continue to pull down the collective reputation of the profession. The majority's job is to keep the boat afloat by doing good work for their clients, day after day, one case at a time.

So even with all you know at this point about preparing and presenting your case at trial, there are some situations in which you should consider hiring an attorney. Here are some scenarios that may make hiring an attorney worth the cost.

♦ **When there is too much at stake.** These cases remind me of investment salespeople on the radio. "How much are you willing to risk?" they ask. Small claims courts in this country hear claims having values up to $25,000. The greater the stakes in the case, the greater the risk of loss for not spending part of it in legal fees.

♦ **When proof of your case is complicated.** In cases of fraud, the swindle may be hard to prove. Here are five elements you need to prove in every fraud case: 1) a false representation; 2) made by a person who knew it was false at the time it was made; 3) with the intent to deceive another person; 4) whom it does in fact deceive; 5) with resulting damages. If there is insufficient proof on any one element, you will lose.

Some schemes and scams are obscure. They must be put together like a puzzle before a judge can be convinced that fraud occurred and the injured party is entitled to recover. Proof of damages in a specific amount can also be difficult in these cases.

Remember, in most states, once fraud is proven, the damaged person is entitled to recover punitive or exemplary damages. These are awarded to punish the deceiver and prevent the conduct from occurring again. The likelihood of a higher damage award in these cases will often offset the cost of hiring a lawyer to pursue this kind of claim.

The same holds true with other legally technical causes of action, such as libel, slander, malicious prosecution, abuse of process, and intentional infliction of emotional distress. (See Appendix 2 on page 163 for definitions. Most of these are so difficult to prove they are excluded from small claims courts. Ask the clerk.) Cases that are basically contract or tort cases can be complicated by the subject matter, such as conversion by manipulation of company records, or proof of personal injuries where there has been a pre-existing medical condition. You can also consider getting representation when the proof of your damages is complicated. You might need assistance to discover every dime of the damages in the first place, and then to put them in a form that a judge can understand.

Not long ago a plaintiff came to my courtroom complaining that his former company had failed to pay him his full commissions for the five years before he left. He had handled more than 1,000 transactions during that time. His proof involved comparing all of his records, which were not complete or well-organized, against his commission check records. The company countered with all its records of the same transactions.

The salesman won, but I am sure he did not win all he was entitled to because he could not prove everything. It is notable that the case took more than four hours to try, trying not only the issues, but also the judge's patience. Had he hired a lawyer, he might have received all that was coming to him, and it would have been easier on everyone involved in the trial. An attorney should have been able to summarize the transactions and prove the salesman's total loss.

♦ **When your case has been "removed" to a court of "superior" jurisdiction.** Superior courts usually have rules of procedure and evidence that only one trained in the law can understand and use effectively.

♦ **When the proof of your case requires experts (especially medical experts).** In order to recover damages for personal injuries, some states require that you have medical testimony to show that your treatment was reasonable and necessary, and that the treatment you received was related to the injury you are complaining about. Getting the facts from psychologists, psychiatrists, and other physicians, actuaries, accident reconstruction experts, chemists, certified public accountants, and engineers of all kinds can be just as challenging.

♦ **If you decide that you just don't want to try your own case after all.** Trying one's own case is not for everybody. You will be no less a valuable person if you turn your case over to a lawyer after you make an informed decision about it. You can still be an asset to your attorney by presenting your case to him or her in an understandable way. It will save both of you time and it will save you money.

♦ **For any other good reason.** If you look back to the chapter on finding sound free legal advice, it should give you some ideas about where to find the best attorney to handle your case when you are willing and able to pay for it.

In choosing an attorney, always try to get a referral. The best source for one would be your family, friends, and business acquaintances. As said elsewhere, lawyers live and die in the legal business on the strength of their reputations. If an attorney did diligent work for one client, it is more likely that the same level of effort will be repeated for others. Shop around. If you talk to a lawyer who does not handle cases like yours, ask him or her to refer you to two or three attorneys who do.

You probably have some time. Most small claims must be brought within two years after the incident occurred. When you contact attorneys, be sure and find out what experience they have, their areas of specialty. Most important, be sure to find out how much they will charge you, based on your brief but complete explanation of what your case is about.

You can go to secondary sources for referrals, such as local or state bar association lawyer referral services, referral services in the yellow pages, or similar call-in services advertised in daily urban newspapers.

When you have had all your major fears quelled about what a particular lawyer will do for you and for how much, get it in writing. If he or she does not offer you a written contract, before the attorney does any substantial work for you, confirm your understanding in a letter to the lawyer.

Once your case is turned over, you may have a great sense of relief. You are still responsible to provide your lawyer with all pertinent facts. As with any service contract, you are buying the lawyer's time, attention, and effort. Be willing to help whenever you can, but without interfering. Any way you can make the attorney's job more efficient will benefit your pocketbook. And insist that you be informed of any significant events or changes. The time a lawyer spends on your case is the lawyer's time, but *your* money.

CHAPTER 16

GOING FOR IT: YOUR FIRST TRIP TO THE COURTHOUSE

So you've tried to resolve your dispute through a settlement, but your opponent has failed to see the advantage of early settlement, and you have decided to file a suit. You have already called the clerk for information and directions to the right courthouse in your town or city. Take your complete file and your checkbook for the filing and service fees. Make sure your file contains all the information you need as explained in the next chapter.

My first trip to a courthouse was like my first day in a new school: I had some vague idea of what I would find there, but no idea what it would actually look like. Once you park, or arrive in the vicinity of the courthouse, the first challenge may be finding the front door. Your immediate goal is to find the clerk's office.

Most urban and suburban courthouses are court *complexes*, housing several courts handling different kinds of cases. For security reasons, there may be only one door leading to the various courts. This leads to the First Rule of Courthouse Exploration: Always ask questions. It saves time. Your time is valuable. (As Benjamin Franklin once said, "Dost thou love life? Then do not squander time, for that is the stuff life is made of.") In rural areas, you may find only one court clerk who handles all the legal business for you precinct or county.

Courthouse personnel will direct you to the small claims court clerk, or at least a directory telling you where this office is. Once you are there, be ready to tell the clerk that you would like to file a small claims action against the defendant, and for how much. The clerk will either supply you with forms or tell you what you need to do to make out your claim in writing. Which brings us back to the First Rule of Courthouse Exploration: Always ask questions.

If you have the luxury of a little additional time, plan to stay a few minutes to observe any small claims trials that might be in progress. The clerk will know which courtrooms are active. These are public trials, so any citizen may visit. In a matter of 15 minutes, you can know the way trials actually happen in your court—how strict or lenient the judge is about rules of evidence, and the formality with which the hearings are conducted. In a few minutes, you can gauge the personality of the judge, knowing that he might hear your case. In smaller towns and cities, it will be likely that there is only one judge, so you will only need to make one such evaluation.

All this preparation will help you enter the courthouse with confidence on the day of your trial, should your case reach that point without a settlement.

CHAPTER 17

FiliNG YOUR
SMAll ClAiMS SuiT

You now have knowledge. And remember, knowledge is power! You also have stern resolve. You are prepared. I cannot emphasize often enough how important it is to talk to the court clerk and others who can provide you with pertinent information. You are on your way to the courthouse and the clerk's office of your court. You are ready to file.

Two minor points: 1) In order to sue, you must be the party interested in the outcome of the case; you cannot represent anyone else's interests unless you are an attorney; and 2) Only a child's parent or legal guardian can pursue a claim on his or her behalf.

Once you are in the office for filing civil claims, let the clerk know what you are doing there. He or she will probably provide you with a form for your statement of claim, complaint, or petition for relief. If not, and you need to make your own, you will need to include the following information:

♦ **Your full name, address, and telephone number.** You will want to be found if the clerk needs to contact you about trial dates or anything else concerning your case. Include your daytime telephone number if there is a place for it on the form. If any of this information changes while your lawsuit is underway, you should write to the clerk. Once your case is filed, it will be given a case number. All of the documents in your case will be kept in the clerk's office in this numbered file. You should get a copy of what you give to the clerk, but if you do not, make sure you have the case number if it is available so you can put it on all correspondence and refer to it in telephone calls.

♦ **The correct name and address of the defendant(s).** Is this silly? No, its very serious. People do business mainly under three different forms: the proprietor, the partnership, and the corporation. If the defendant is a business, the correct name and form of business is important, because if you sue the wrong business entity, your case might be dismissed without any fight, although you will not lose your right to file your case again against the right party. If you sue in the wrong city or county, you may be able to have the case transferred to the right court, but it would delay your case. The power of any court is limited to a specific geographic area, precinct, district, city, or county. A process server cannot go to a post office box. Get a street address.

What if the person or party you want to sue lives in another state? No problem. Every state has a *Long Arm Statute,* so named because it allows the long arm of the court in your state to reach into other states and grab people into your court. In order for someone to be grabbed brought into the courts of your state, there must be have been some significant contact between you and the person in your state. For example, a motor vehicle collision may have occurred in your state, or a contract may have been signed there.

Suing the individual or business proprietor. The proprietor is an individual who owns a business. In order to properly bring him or her into court, you need a full name and *residence* address. An individual can only be sued in certain places, and the county of residence is usually the primary place. To be sure, bring all the addresses you know for this individual. If you can have the defendant served in more than one place, the process server will have an easier job. If you learn that the person resides in a county or city other than yours, ask the clerk if you can sue in yours because of the kind of case you have.

If you are suing two or more defendants, no matter what business form(s) they operate under, if one defendant is properly within the geographical boundaries of the court, there is a way to bring the others into the same court. Again, ask the clerk.

If you are suing a business and do not know the owner's name or what business form it operates under, you need to find out! Your secretary of state will tell you if it is or is not a corporation, and you can find out who owns a business by calling or going to examine the business license in your local business license office. In some states, business names or trade names are indexed in the city or county records. These give the business name and the name and address of the person or corporation doing business under each name.

Suing a partnership. Under general partnership law, if you serve any partner with the papers, the partnership is properly sued, and you get a judgment, it will be against the whole partnership. To be successful, though, you must show that you are suing a partnership on your court papers. Your naming of the defendant would read something like: "Mike Savage, a Partner of Happy Trails, Ltd., A Partnership."

A *Limited Partnership* is a business created where a bunch of investors (limited partners) turn over their cash to a general or managing partner to invest or manage. If you dealt contrarily with a limited partnership, the general or managing partner should be sued where he or she lives, and the partnership named in the papers. Many states have recently created another type of partnership, a *Limited Liability Partnership*. If your search of business records shows that your potential defendant is one of these, your lawsuit may be subject to different rules about who needs to get the court papers. One other, the *Professional Association,* may exist in your state and also be subject to special rules.

Suing the corporation. As stated previously, corporations are fictitious legal entities. They are ghosts, legal entities that exist solely because the state legislature has said they do. Like parents take care of their children, states take care of their corporations. So suing one is a little more technical. When you sue a corporation, you name the corporation you are suing as a defendant, for example, "XYZ Corporation," but you direct service to one of the people who are part of the corporation.

Corporations only exist through their individual officers, agents, or employees. Only a few of these can be served with suit papers to properly get the corporation in court. As a general rule, only those people who have a management-level job can be served with legal papers for the company. In each state there will be a person named in the corporation papers on file with the secretary of state who is the person available to be served court papers; this is the *agent for service*. Usually it's a lawyer. The president or chief executive officer can also be served.

Remember, everyone, including fictional legal persons, has a right to notice, and it is assumed that if even a minor corporate manager is served with legal papers, it is likely that he will contact the higher-ups in the company about it.

The rule in most states is that you can successfully bring a corporation into court by suing any of these people in any county where the corporation has a principle place of business or where the office of the agent for service is. Again, the clerk will know.

♦ **A clear, concise, and complete statement of your claim.** This is done in the body of your statement of claim or complaint. If you can state it in one sentence, great. Use one paragraph at most. If you have more than one claim, write a separate sentence or paragraph for each.

♦ **How much you are suing for in each claim, as well as the total.** This is known as the *ad damnum* clause. Remember, the total amount cannot be above the maximum you can sue for in your small claims court. You do not need to state how you calculated the amount of damages you are seeking. That can be left for trial.

♦ **Your complete signature.** Your local rules may require that it be signed or sworn to and signed before the clerk, so ask before you sign. Make sure that you print your name legibly under your signature, so there is no problem knowing who you are if you need to be contacted at any point in the process.

Once you have provided all this information, pay the filing and service fees. Don't worry, the clerk will let you know how much. Get a copy of what you just filed.

WAIT! Before you leave, ask if the clerk has any rules or guides available explaining procedures in that court. Many have brochures that will give you the nuts and bolts, as well as tactics to avoid danger and pitfalls. Once you get this information, read it. It will be invaluable.

What Happens Next

The clerk will keep the original of your Statement of Claim or Complaint in the court file, and send a copy to the marshal, constable, or sheriff to be served on the defendant(s). A *summons* will be attached to the claim sheet. The summons says, in effect, "You are being sued. You only have a short time (usually between 10 and 30 days, depending on local rules) to respond by filing an Answer or Counterclaim. If you fail to respond within that time a judgment will be taken against you." In other words, if the defendant doesn't respond, he or she will automatically lose.

If the process server, who will serve the defendant with the summons and a copy of the Statement of Claim or Complaint, cannot locate any person you have asked to have served, the clerk will let you know. You may need to investigate further to get a current or better address.

Get Your Subpoenas!

Before you leave the clerk's office, if you are planning to call any witnesses during your trial besides yourself, get subpoenas for each of them. *Subpoena* means "under penalty." A subpoena tells the witness, "Come to court, or else," and puts the power of the court behind it to force an appearance in case he or she is reluctant or shy.

Your witnesses may be your friends or relatives, but they may not be available to testify if they need to work, or if they "just don't feel like it" that day. A subpoena will excuse them from work, school, or almost everything except emergency surgery or death. Even though you may trust that your brother or best friend will show up in court if you ask him to, be sure with a subpoena.

Ask the clerk three final questions:

1. "How do I properly get these subpoenas served on my witnesses?"
2. "Do I need to notify you before trial that a witness has been subpoenaed?"
3. "What do you I do if the subpoenaed witness doesn't show up?"

With subpoenas you can force people to come to court because you need them as witnesses and require them to bring evidence to court that you need for your case, but cannot get otherwise. This second kind of subpoena, a *subpoena for the production of documents and things* (or *subpoena duces tecum*), will get both the witness and the documents or other things you need as exhibits into court. There may be a charge for the subpoenas; you may want to wait until you know exactly how many you will need before getting them from the clerk. Usually, this can be handled by mail. Before you leave, ask the clerk if the subpoenaed witnesses are entitled to any fee for the inconvenience of coming to court. Witness fees are usually minimal, but must be offered or paid if you want the judge to enforce the subpoena by bringing your witness to court involuntarily.

If a subpoenaed witness fails to appear in court and is essential for you to prove your case, the judge can either postpone the trial to give you a chance to get your witness there, or send a court officer, a sheriff, or constable to secure the attendance of the witness by any means necessary. Yes, these people, ordinarily large of stature, can even use their handcuffs.

What If *You* Are Sued?

If you are sued, the very first thing to do is read the summons thoroughly. It will tell you how long you have before you need to do anything. But if it says you need to do something, such as respond or appear in court within 10 days, you must, or you may lose all your rights to contest the plaintiff's claim. If you mail your response, it must be in the clerk's office within the time allowed.

The next important point to remember is that you shouldn't panic. All those nasty things the plaintiff said about you in the Statement of Claim or Complaint are just allegations, just bare assertions. The Complaint is not proof of anything except that someone has sued you for what they *say* is a legal claim. The plaintiff must prove it.

Your formal written response to the Summons and the Complaint or Statement of Claim that comes with it is formally known as your *Answer*. It can take many forms depending on your position in the case. Whichever form it takes, once you file it, you should send a copy to the plaintiff at the address listed on the Complaint or Statement of Claim. The clerk should do this also, but you do not want to take the chance on a delay of your trial because the plaintiff did not get a copy of your response.

Some possible responses are as follows:

When the plaintiff is right. If there is no legal reason for you not to pay the full amount that the plaintiff has sued for, you can admit it in your Answer. If you act quickly, you can still prevent a judgment being entered against you by contacting the plaintiff to negotiate a settlement. You can take the position with plaintiff that you will not contest the claim if you are allowed to pay a little less or in installments. If you agree before the time is up for you to file an Answer, you and the plaintiff can enter a Consent Agreement, or Consent Order. You can adapt the ones in the Forms section in Chapter 24. As you can see by their terms, no judgment will be taken against you as long as you live up to the agreement. The advantage gained by this is that your credit report will not show a judgment against you. Local and national credit reporting agencies regularly monitor who loses lawsuits by having judgments entered against them. Adverse judgments are not good for your credit rating.

Even if you do not have time to negotiate, you can still admit the claim in your Answer. Even though the plaintiff will be entitled to an immediate judgment against you, nothing in the legal system is immediate. You can still contact the plaintiff to work out a payment plan after you file your Answer.

It's to the plaintiff's advantage not to have to take extra steps to collect a judgment if you agree to pay it on certain terms, and then actually do it. You simply need to get your Consent Agreement or Order to the judge before the judgment that results from the admission in the Answer is signed by the judge and filed by the clerk. This may take one to two weeks after the Answer filing deadline.

When the plaintiff is right, won't take payments, but you can't pay it all now. Put this in your Answer. In many small claims courts, judges can order that judgments be paid in installments. You may be asked to go to court to briefly explain your circumstances, but it could be worth it. If a judgment for the full amount is entered against you, you could be unhappily surprised by having your bank account seized, part of your wages taken through a garnishment proceeding, or your car disappear from your driveway—all of which are means judgment creditors can take to collect the judgment. Other ways court winners can collect are discussed in Chapter 22.

When you owe some, but not all of what the plaintiff claims. In your Answer, write it out. For example, "I owe her some money, but not as much as she claims." If it ends up in trial, the plaintiff will still have to prove how much you owe. This could happen when the plaintiff has just asked for too much, or because you have a claim against the plaintiff that partially offsets her claim. If you have a right to set off part of the claim, you will need to state in at least one sentence why and how much you say you are entitled to subtract. At trial, you will first need to prove your right to have a subtraction, and then prove the specific amount.

When you owe the plaintiff something, but the plaintiff owes you more. This is just like the last example, but your claim against the plaintiff is larger than the plaintiff's claim against you, so you want the court to wipe out the plaintiff's claim and give you a judgment for the difference. If the judge decides the plaintiff's claim is groundless, or it fails because the plaintiff doesn't prove it, you can win and collect all of your claim.

A defendant with a counterclaim against the plaintiff's claim wears two hats, and one defensive. He is required to defend against the claims of the plaintiff and then switch hats, go on the offensive, and prove a right to recover from the plaintiff, and how much he believes he is entitled to.

When you owe the plaintiff nothing, but you have a whopping claim against him. Simply write, "Plaintiff's claim is denied." Then state your claim. This claim you have against the plaintiff is your *Counterclaim*. After you state in your Answer why you are not indebted to the plaintiff, just as if you were the person filing the suit initially, you should write out the basis of your claim against the plaintiff in a succinct but complete way, and ask for the specific amount you think you are entitled to from the plaintiff. Your evidence will prove your right to recover, and the amount. Again, with your counterclaim, you need to produce enough believable evidence to convince the judge that the plaintiff is liable to you, and the specific degree to which you were damaged—your *damages*.

When you owe the plaintiff's claim, but somebody else is responsible for all or some of it. This does not happen often, but can, in both contract and tort cases.

Wellington put a rebuilt carburetor in Jennings' car and gave him a 30-day warranty. On the last day of the warranty, the carburetor went bad at 2 a.m. while Jennings was 75 miles from the nearest town. Jennings sued for the $125 cost of repair, plus the $95 towing bill.

When Jennings sued Wellington, Wellington agreed to pay some of the damages, but also claimed that Murphy, who had sold Wellington the rebuilt carb, should pay some too.

So Wellington brought Murphy into court by filing a *Third Party Complaint* against him. (See Chapter 24 for a sample "Third Party Complaint" form, as well as other forms you will need.)

Something similar could also happen in a tort case. Let's take a look. Bodkin bought an ax from Jack's Hardware. While using it a short time later, the head came off and caused Bodkin a nasty cut. When Bodkin sued Jack, Jack brought the ax manufacturer into court, because he felt the manufacturer should be at least partially responsible—maybe even fully responsible—for the damage to Bodkin.

Again, this is a matter the court clerk should know by heart, and he or she will give you the what and wherefore to get this done.

When the plaintiff is just flat out wrong. Just deny it. Writing something like "I deny everything the plaintiff claims" will work.

Any time you file an Answer, you can assert any of the defenses mentioned in the chapters on contracts, torts, or combinations of the two, depending on what kind of case it is. The plaintiff usually does not need to respond to a counterclaim until trial.

Counterclaim or not, when you are served with legal process notifying you that you have been sued, *you must do something!* If you fail to do anything or just ignore the summons, a judgment could be entered against you by *default*. You will lose without even playing.

When no response is filed to a Complaint or Statement of Claim within the time allowed, the defendant loses the right to contest the suit, and may lose the right to be notified of any further action in the case. In most cases, judges are authorized to issue a judgment for the amount sued for when the case is stated clearly in the Complaint, and there is a clear right to recover a specific sum of money.

If there is any question about the nature of the case or the amount sued for, the plaintiff may be notified to appear to testify about how the amount sued for was calculated. In some courts, the defendant may be notified also to argue and present evidence against the plaintiff on the sole issue of how much the plaintiff should recover. In these cases, the only question is how much the plaintiff win should. The plaintiff's right to win is established by the defendant's failure to respond to the Summons and Complaint.

Calling the plaintiff to court to prove damages is likely to happen where the amount of damages is uncertain because of the kind of case it is. If the plaintiff sues for "$2,000 for pain and suffering," the calculation of the damage is so subjective, a judge will probably want to know how the plaintiff decided on that figure for these *unliquidated damages*.

Where the amount of damages is fixed and specific, or *liquidated*, as in "$350 due on account for 100 pieces of lumber at $3.50 each," a hearing will not be required. Plaintiff wins without a fight! Seems a little deflating to me.

Assuming the defendant has at least filed an Answer, the case will move toward trial. If you fail to settle your case before trial (be sure to let the clerk know if you do), the clerk will notify you of a trial date.

Discovery

Between the time an Answer is filed and the trial, many courts have a set period for you to find out about what the other side intends to prove at the trial, and for them to find out about your claim. This process is called *discovery*, and the forms and procedures you can use should be explained in the court's rules or procedure manual you picked up from the clerk earlier.

The rules of discovery usually allow the parties to submit written questions to each other to be answered under oath, file requests to examine documents or other evidence that a party expects to produce at the trial, and to produce the list of witnesses the other party expects to have at the trial. The rules of discovery vary widely in the different courts throughout the country. They can be helpful in getting information for you to assess the strengths and weaknesses of your case against the opposing party's. The more information you have, the easier it will be for you to reach a favorable settlement or to predict a trial outcome.

Discovery or not, you are now fully on your way in this adventure!

CHAPTER 18

A Tour of The Courthouse

"Ladies and Gentlemen, welcome to our little courtroom. My name is Johnson Abernathy. I am a bailiff in this court.

"As we enter, you may first notice the leather high-backed chair way up at the other end of the room. Notice that it is elevated. This is where the judge sits, and from where great judicious pronouncements are made in this court. The chair is way up there so that even our shortest judge will appear to be imposing and full of authority.

"To the judge's right, to our left as we face the judge from the back of the room, and one level down, you can see a chair with a microphone in front of it. You can't see it from here, but on the counter in front of that chair rests a Gideon's Bible. Before each witness begins to testify in a trial, he or she is asked to place the left hand on the bible and take an oath to tell the truth. Most of the time, it works.

"Immediately in front of the judge, on the lowest, or floor level, you see a chair for the courtroom clerk. The clerk is in charge of all the papers filed in a lawsuit, the list of cases to be handled in court each day, and the organization and safekeeping of documents and other evidence submitted during a trial.

"To the clerk's right sits the court reporter. Using a special court stenographic machine or a tape recorder, the reporter makes a record of everything that is said during a trial. This can be transcribed later in case the parties want to appeal or if they want a copy of the trial for their records.

"Because this is a small claims court, the court does not supply a court reporter to you. If you want your case transcribed for any reason, you will need to arrange to have a court reporter here and arrange to pay him or her. Any certified court reporter will likely do a good job for you. You can find listings for them in our local yellow pages.

"To our right, against the wall, you can see two rows of seven evenly spaced chairs. They look that way not because we're especially neat. They are bolted to the floor. These are for the jurors, either six or 12, and for alternate jurors who hear cases on stand-by in case a regular juror gets sick.

"The parties and their lawyers, if they have them, sit at the two tables facing the judge. The short partition wall behind these tables is the *bar*. There's a bar in every courtroom. When our system of laws was brought over from England in the 1600s, no one except those admitted to the bar—barristers or solicitors—could be in front of that wall. It was thought that separation from the common people was good. This separation was supposed to help maintain the dignity of the court.

"What do *I* do? The bailiff's lot is not an easy one. My mantle is heavy with responsibility. I am in charge of making sure everyone who participates in court, the parties and witnesses, know where they're supposed to be. I am charged with keeping order in the courtroom and protecting the jurors. I enforce the 'no hats, gum, or bikinis in the courtroom' rules.

"My most obvious duty is to shout in my best *basso profundo*, 'All rise!' when the judge comes in.

"The rows of seats behind the bar are for spectators. Trials are public throughout this country, and anyone who likes can come watch. If there are people in these seats during your trial, they will usually be parties, witnesses, and an occasional lawyer waiting for their cases to be heard. They may want to see how the trial of another case works before it is their turn.

"This concludes our tour. Are there any questions?

"Oh, that's Judge Henry Brundage hanging on the wall. He was the first chief judge of this court. He died in 1983. I've heard that when he was sitting for that portrait, as dour as he looks, it was the first time anybody had ever seen him smile.

"Thank you for your kind attention. If you will follow me, I will show you where the clerk's office is. They will be able answer any questions you have about how to file, pursue, or defend a case in this court. And you can call the clerks later for answers to those questions that pop into your heads while driving home this afternoon."

Part IV

Trial Notebook

CHAPTER 19

PRIMER: ANATOMY of a TRIAL

You have done all you can do, including your best effort to settle your case on the courthouse steps. The culmination of all your effort is at hand. Preparation is over and it is time for the moment of truth. You are going to try your case before a judge. You are on time and appropriately dressed.

But wait! There are still a few things it will be helpful to know. The following will help you create a trial notebook, a step-by-step outline for the presentation of your case.

If you are a plaintiff, or a defendant asserting a counterclaim, you need to prove two things: first, that you are entitled to recover, and second, in what amount. All your success rests upon proof of these two matters. You will do this through your testimony, the testimony of your other witnesses and by showing the judge your exhibits. (Remember, *showing* is better than telling.)

If you are a defendant, you need to show that the plaintiff is not entitled to win anything, or if the plaintiff is going to win, that it will be for the least possible amount. Technically, you do not need to prove a thing, but never leave it up to the plaintiff to fail. As in a game, a good defense is your best offense.

A trial is like any sales pitch. You tell the audience what you are going to show, you show it, and then you tell the audience what they saw. Your pitch should be a convincing story that persuades your audience that you have been wronged and that shows them how they can make it right.

A quick reminder about the rules of evidence: These rules are technical legal rules, which may be enforced to a greater or lesser degree by your particular judge. The rules control what facts are considered by the judge during a trial. They exist to assure that the facts considered are only those that are trustworthy, worthy of belief. So, your witnesses' testimonies should be direct and clear, and your exhibits must be what you say they are.

Some judges allow the parties to present all the evidence that they want at trial. The judge then mentally sifts through it all to separate the believable from the questionable. Other judges will hear nothing that is fishy or capable of corrupting the truth.

Regardless of publicity to the contrary, the goal of any legal investigation, such as a trial, is the discovery of the truth. The judge wants to hear what really happened to see if there is a legal basis for adjusting the controversy between the parties. Your success will hinge on how well you can recreate that truth for the judge.

In the beginning, before you present any testimony, you may have a chance to make an opening statement. Its purpose is to let the judge know the particular cause of action that has brought you to court—the what, when, how, where, and why—and to summarize what you expect your evidence to prove. The defendant has a chance to respond by briefly summarizing his or her case. Each opening statement should be brief and succinct, and touch only the most important points. It should be one minute, max.

When the trial actually starts, the plaintiff, who has the burden of proving his or her side of the case, goes first by testifying or calling the first witness. You may ask specific questions of your witnesses, or just ask each to tell the judge what he or she knows about the dispute. After each witness testifies, the other party has the opportunity to *cross-examine* the witness. The purpose of cross-examination is to test the witness's believability.

On cross-examination, you must ask questions—do not argue with the witness, comment on the witness's testimony, or try to testify yourself while the witness is on the stand. Your questions should be geared toward getting yes or no answers from the witness, such as, *"Isn't it true* that at the time you say you saw the collision, you were actually in an impassioned embrace with your boyfriend, George, under the street light?" "Contrary to what you just testified to, *didn't you* tell the police officer at the scene that it was your fault?" As in other aspects of trial preparation, you will need to plan and maybe practice forming questions this way. (More on cross-examination later.)

The plaintiff will proceed through his or her case in this fashion until all of his or her witnesses have testified. Then it will be the defendant's turn to do the same—testify and call all witnesses to defend against the plaintiff's claim and to assert any counterclaims.

When the defendant is finished, if there is a counterclaim in the case, the judge may permit the plaintiff a little time to have witnesses testify in *rebuttal* to the counterclaim evidence. Plaintiffs: Be bold! At the end of the defendant's side of the case, ask the judge if you can offer rebuttal evidence. Its purpose is to attack or undermine the proof that the defendant has offered. When it appears that the defendant is finished, the judge may ask, "Is there anything else?" or something similar. Your answer should be, "Yes, your honor, I would like to offer evidence against the counterclaim," or, "Yes, I would like to offer evidence in rebuttal."

After both sides have had all their witnesses testify and have shown the judge all the exhibits in the case, you may have a chance to give a final or closing argument. Its purpose is to convince the judge that what he or she has just seen entitles you to win. Build up your side and tear down the other side. Stress your strong points and minimize or argue away their strong points.

And remember: Win or lose, you've done all you can to put yourself in the best position to win. You have done all any high-priced attorney could have done for you. Congratulations!

Chapter 20

Final Trial Preparation

You now have a general idea of the direction, ebb, and flow of a trial. This chapter will give you the nuts and bolts of putting your case in a form that a judge will appreciate, enjoy, and most of all, *believe*.

1. Opening Statement. The judge knows nothing about your case. Her only concern is that the case be heard fully and fairly. The parties should be treated as equals, with dignity and respect, whether they are represented by a lawyer or not.

In a one-minute opening statement, you can tell the judge everything she needs to know to decide in your favor. This is your first chance to show the judge you are right and should win. Start with a one-sentence summary: "This case is about a contract the defendant failed to live up to and I will show that I am entitled to $_____ because she didn't. The evidence will show..."

Then state your case in one paragraph that gives the when, what, who, where, how, and sometimes why. Pinpoint the time, place, chief characters, and the major actions of these players in the real-life drama that brought you to court. It is the first chance to persuade the judge that your cause is just and true. So emphasize your strong points, minimize the weak. Most of all, give it life!

At the end, add (in your own words), "Judge, I believe that after you have heard all the evidence in this case, you will conclude that I am entitled to a judgment in the amount of $_____ plus the court costs."

Defendants: "Judge, I believe that after you have heard all the evidence, you will conclude that the plaintiff has not proven her case, and I am entitled to a judgment for the defense." If you have a counterclaim, add, "...and further, I am entitled to recover $_____ on my counterclaim."

Then comes the presentation of the evidence in the case, through witnesses and exhibits.

2. Witnesses. Witnesses, including yourself, are people who know something about your case. It is your job to limit what they tell the judge to what they know about it. There is a whole lot that you and your other witnesses may know. Stick to the stuff that relates directly to your case. This way, your evidence will be both "relevant" and "material."

Before you get to the courthouse, you should talk to each witness. Most people are scared of being in a courthouse, let alone on a witness stand. Let them know what you are going to ask them about.

If you are going to give them exhibits to identify and to testify about, tell them which ones and show the exhibits to your witnesses. Point out to them what you think is important, and what you intend to ask about each document or exhibit.

As you talk to them, find out what they will say in their testimony. If it is different from what the witness has told you before, let him or her know. But never, never, *never* tell a witness what to say!

The most important reason you preview their testimony is so that you are not surprised by what they say under oath from the witness stand. It could upset your whole trial plan. Minor inconsistencies are sure to show up, but make sure your witnesses will testify as you expect them to on your major points. Ask them not to chew gum or tobacco while they are testifying.

Ask them to testify only about things they observed themselves, not about what someone else told them about the facts. Statements given by people who are not available to testify as witnesses are *hearsay*. Hearsay statements are bad evidence, because they cannot be tested by cross-examination and are not made under oath. Since there is no way they can be tested to see if they are true or false, they do nothing to further the truth-finding process. If the other side's witnesses start talking about what someone else told them, who is not there to testify, it is your place to stand up and say firmly, "Your honor, I object! That statement is hearsay. Because there is no way to test whether it is true or not, it should not be a part of what you consider in this case." (More on objections later.)

Let your witnesses know that when they step up to the witness stand, someone will place them under oath to tell "the truth, the whole truth, and nothing but the truth."

Let them know that they will be cross-examined by the other party. When they are, they should listen to each question carefully and answer it, without volunteering other information. Make sure they let the questioner know if any question is not understood. It is their testimony and they are entitled to tell it as clearly as they can. "I don't understand the question," works.

If a cross-examination question calls for a yes or no answer, instruct your witness to answer the question with one of these one-word answers, then explain their answer as much as they think is necessary. It is okay, as long as they are still answering the question. There is no such thing as a simple yes or no answer. If you and your witnesses explain your responses, it will keep you from being backed into a corner by a tricky questioner. By this method, witnesses, and not the person who is asking them questions, will control the way their testimony comes out.

All of this will help you and each of your witnesses relax. To get the maximum benefit, you and your witnesses must be believed. A trained judge will look at and listen to testimony with an eye and ear toward how witnesses present themselves, the direct way they tell their stories, the probability or improbability of what they say, and any obvious biases witnesses show. Remember, if there are any inconsistencies (and there usually are), the judge must choose whom to believe.

Ask your witnesses to be on time, sober, neatly dressed (so that not too much skin shows), and without too much makeup or flashy jewelry. Tell each to ask someone in the courthouse for help if they cannot find you or the courtroom when they get there. Carpool if you can.

In the Trial Notebook forms that follow, you will see several for witnesses, including a section for the exhibits you want each witness to testify about. I suggest that you *not* write out every question you want to ask. You will not always get the exact answer you expect, and your script will not match what is happening in the courtroom. This will interrupt the flow of the witness's story. Better to just list the facts you want the witness to bring out, then check each off mentally or actually in your notebook when he or she testifies to each fact. Make sure every necessary fact you need from each witness is checked off before he or she leaves the witness stand.

You may get a chance to ask your witness a few questions after the other party has cross-examined him or her. The purpose of this *redirect examination* is to clear up testimony that has been muddled, confused, or undermined by the questions asked by your opponent during cross-examination. If you need to do damage control, and it looks as if the judge is anticipating your calling your next witness, simply ask, "Judge, may I ask my witness a few questions on redirect examination?" You should hear, "Of course you can, but be brief."

Whom should you call first?

Probably yourself. You have already introduced yourself to the judge in your opening statement. On the other hand, if you have many witnesses, you may want to testify last to fill in any gaps that your witnesses have left, or to clear up any confusion. When you testify, take anything with you that you want the judge to see as part of your case—those exhibits you want to introduce during your testimony.

If you have not been asked to give an opening statement, give it first in your testimony. Again, sell the judge on your version of things early. Jury studies show that most jurors make up their minds about a case in the first 10 minutes. I have not seen any studies on this, but I suspect that judges' decisions are based disproportionately on what they hear during the first 10 minutes, too. Let the judge have it, and don't let up throughout your trial until you are done and you have won.

Call the rest of your witnesses in chronological order, the first witness testifying about what happened first and so forth, or call them in some other order that makes sense. The order could depend on a pattern of how they became involved in your case, or it may depend on the exhibits you want them to identify and explain.

You are recreating history here, and you want to present it in a way that first will be understood, then wholeheartedly believed!

If you have any witnesses that you are calling because they are experts at what they do, you need to let the judge know how they came to be experts. Before these *expert witnesses* tell what they know about your case, ask them about their background. Try something like this:

"Your honor, as my next witness, I call Mack Kaley."

(Mr. Kaley comes up, is seated in the witness chair, and the clerk gives him the oath to tell the truth.)

Q. Please state your name for the judge.

A. My name is Mack Kaley.

Q. What kind of work do you do Mr. Kaley?

A. I am the owner and operator of Kaley's Automotive over on the Rome Highway.

Q. What kind of work do you do there?

A. We do all kinds of repair work on all kinds of cars and trucks.

Q. How long have you been repairing cars?

A. Oh, since I was 14—about 42 years.

Q. Do you have any special training?

A. I and all my mechanics are A.S.E. certified, and we get recertified every three years. We have the most up-to-date diagnostic and repair equipment in our shop, and I constantly keep updated on new products and techniques by reading the major trade journals.

Q. So the judge knows, what does A.S.E. stand for?

A. It stands for Automotive Standards of Excellence. It is an independent testing and certification organization that maintains the standards for auto repair throughout the industry.

Q. Do you remember last June when I asked you to look at my 1993 Plymouth Acclaim?

A. Like it was yesterday. (He smiles broadly.)

Q. Tell the judge what you saw and what you did.

As you can see, the series of questions begins by showing the judge why he or she should consider this witness an expert. It also identifies the subject about which the witness has the special education, training, or experience necessary to be an expert. So when the expert testifies, the judge will have a basis for believing his opinion. In the case above, the questioner is leading up to asking Mr. Kaley his opinion about why a car broke down.

Should you call the other party as a witness? Most court procedural rules allow you to do this. Don't, unless you cannot prove a particular fact adequately through your own witnesses. But they will not be friendly witnesses.

If you do call the other party, be sure that you ask the judge if you may call him or her for the purpose of cross-examination. Say, "Your honor, may I call Mr. Balfour, the plaintiff, for the limited purpose of cross-examination?" Ask those yes-or-no cross-examination questions. Remember, you will have a chance to ask questions again if your opponent testifies on his or her side of the case.

Introduce each of your witnesses, except for your opponent, to the judge. Ask the person's name, where he or she lives, and how he or she came to be in a position of knowing something about this case. Then you can ask what the witness knows about it—the who, what, when, where, and why of what he knows. For example:

Q. Please state you name for the judge.

A. Fred Finestone.

Q. Where do you live, Mr. Finestone?

A. In Dallas, Georgia.

Q. Mr. Finestone, do you remember the night last June when you were riding in my car and we had an accident?

A. Like it was yesterday. (He snickers nervously and glances over at the judge to see if she is amused.)

Q. Where were you sitting?

A. In the back seat with my wife, Else.

Q. Tell the judge what you saw and heard.

After Fred tells everything he has to say about how the collision occurred, who was at fault, and what damage he observed, ask him, and all the rest of your witnesses, the clean-up question, "Is there anything that you think is important that I did not ask you?"

How many witnesses should you have? Enough so the judge hears the complete story only once. If two witnesses standing on the same street corner see the same accident, and they are prepared to testify that they saw exactly the same thing, only one of them is needed. The judge won't want to hear the story retold. The retelling would be *cumulative* testimony. It just accumulates; it doesn't add anything to your story.

Because the stories of any two people who experience the same events will overlap, you can expect that some of your testimony and witnesses' testimony will too, but there should be at least one important fact a witness can testify to that no others will.

There is an exception to this suggestion. When you are your only witness, but there is another one who has significant knowledge of the facts of your case, you may use that witness to back up what you have told the judge. In the Fred Finestone example, you can expect that Fred will testify to just about the same facts as the party who has called him as a witness. Fred's testimony will be a little different, because he viewed the incident from the back seat, but all the other essential facts should be the same. His testimony will add believability to the plaintiff's testimony.

If any of your friends or family would like to come watch your trial, they are free to do so. Trials are public. Don't worry about there being a jeering crowd in the courtroom while you are trying your own case. Anyone who is there is there for business. The occasional scout troop or school class will not disrupt you. Besides, you have a more important audience you are trying to impress: the judge.

Your judge may turn out to be more than just a passive audience. Many ask questions during and at the end of witnesses' testimonies. You generally cannot tell which way a judge will decide based on these questions. The judge is just curious. If you are questioned by the judge, answer him or her as you would a question from anyone. Even if it seems to you as if the judge's questions may be favoring the other side, don't be contemptuous! It's the last comment, a judgment in your favor, that is the important one.

3. Exhibits. Exhibits are everything you want the judge to see except the witnesses: photographs, letters, contracts, canceled checks, receipts, books of account, car parts, doctor bills. But the only way the judge will know that the exhibit relates to your case is for a witness to testify how it does.

Getting your judge to consider your exhibit as part of the case is a two-step process. First, you demonstrate that the thing is what you say it is, that it is *authentic* or *genuine*. For example, the canceled check you present is actually the one you used to pay the defendant for the item you bought before you had to throw it on the scrap heap; the photograph you want the judge to look at is a good picture—it accurately shows the conditions that existed at the time the photo was taken; your diagram accurately depicts the scene of the accident; the oil you have in the jar in court is what the mechanic sold you as transmission fluid. So you tell what the item is or have your witness do so.

Some questions you might ask the witness include:

"Ms. Witness, let me show you this and ask you if you can identify it."
"What is it?"
"Who prepared it?"
"It is it accurate?"

These questions show the judge how the thing came to be and how it is related to the case. In legal parlance, this is known as "laying a foundation."

You must "introduce into evidence" each item you want the judge to consider as part of your case. The judge will be seeing it for the first time, so introductions are proper. After the witness has identified what it is, ask the judge if you can show it to him or her at that time. The judge may want to give the other party a chance to look at your item to see if they object to the judge's looking at it.

Remember, because a witness's memory will tend to fade over time, and some witnesses may actually not tell the truth on purpose, exhibits tend to tell "the whole truth and nothing but the truth" better than witnesses can. You have chosen your witnesses because each of them knows something about your case that other people do not, and you want them to tell the judge what they know about it to your advantage. Exhibits are stronger proof than testimony, so if you have items that relate to your case, the testimony of a witness who testifies about an exhibit will strengthen the credibility of that witness. He or she will be more believable.

We receive 80 percent of the information we get through our sense of sight, so exhibits are strong evidence. Exhibits can be documents, other writings, or other representations on paper that reveal information about your case. Or they can be the very thing you want the judge to examine: the garment you say the dry cleaner ruined, a cheap window shutter for which you were charged the exclusive-grade price, the scars on your arm where your neighbor's cat scratched you, and the like. As long as it relates to the case, and can be presented simply without endangering anyone, almost anything that is helpful to explain your case to the judge can be brought in as an exhibit. But be reasonable. A good photograph of the rust holes in the "new" muffler you bought is more practical than bringing your entire exhaust system to court.

If your exhibit is a document, it should be the original document, or you or your witness should be able to explain why it is not the original. This is known as *The Best Evidence Rule*, a technical rule of evidence that may or may not be enforced in your court, but be ready. If the question comes up, in most courts, it will be adequate if you explain why you do not have the original: You cannot expect to have the original of a letter you sent to the other party. But if you can get an original document before trial, you should.

Reminder: A document, such as an estimate of damage, that is prepared by someone who is not there to testify about it may not become part of your case, because it is *hearsay*. If the document is essential to your case, subpoena the witness to identify and explain it. A police report is information others have told the officer, and therefore also hearsay. But because they are official documents created by professionals, they may be admissible anyway. Find out.

Also, do not make marks or notes on any document you want the judge to see that were not there originally. A marking that you put there in preparation for trial that highlights any part of a document may make it so unfair to the other side that the judge will refuse to look at it. The exception to this is when you mark your exhibits in preparation for trial.

You can create charts, maps, diagrams, and summaries of your other evidence, as long as it helps the judge understand what really happened. As with any exhibit, you or your witness should explain briefly how the exhibit came to be—that the diagram of a motor vehicle collision was drawn after returning to the scene the next day, that a sales chart was generated by comparing the sales figures directly from the books, etc. After the judge learns how the exhibit came to exist, then the witness can go ahead and relate what is important about the exhibit.

The same principles apply to computer printouts. Computer calculations are assumed to be as accurate as the information put into them.

When you look at your Trial Notebook witness forms in Chapter 21, let them serve as an outline for each point you want each witness to testify about. Once you have these forms completed, you should be able to see your game plan to victory spread out before you.

Once you have decided on the order in which you will present your exhibits, you should mark them, "P-1" for plaintiff's first exhibit, or "D-1" if you are the defendant. Mark them in an area that does not obscure what the exhibit is there to show. If it is a document, write the exhibit number in a top corner or on the back. If you do this before trial, the judge will be impressed. It is more than most attorneys do. And it is very helpful when there are many exhibits, so that you, and more importantly, the judge, can keep track of them.

Remember, in order for you to make each exhibit part of the facts the judge will weigh in deciding your case, you must ask the judge to use it. Again, say, "Your honor, I would like to offer Exhibit P-1 into evidence." If you have not done it before you ask the judge to consider the exhibit, you should let the other side see what you are offering to the judge. If the other side does not successfully object, and you have shown what the exhibit is and how it relates to your case, the judge should allow it to be part of the case, that is, among the facts the judge will consider in rendering the judgment. If you forget to put an exhibit into evidence, the judge is prohibited by law from considering it on the way to making the decision in your case. So, do it.

When a lawyer represents the other side, you can expect that he or she will, at some point in the middle of your case, jump up and say, "Your honor, I object! That evidence is irrelevant and immaterial!" When this happens, explain to the judge how you have shown that your item of evidence is authentic, how it relates to your case (relevance), and how it tends to prove a fact you are trying to show (materiality).

If your judge agrees with the opposing lawyer on any point, ask the judge for the basis of the ruling. If the judge says, "Sustained," ask the judge what that means in terms of what you are trying to do at that point in your case. There will be more on the what and why of objections in the next section. Once you see how objections work, you will see better how to react against them if they are tried on you.

4. Objections. Two can play the game of "Objection!" You can play, win, and have a great time at it.

During your opponent's presentation, he or she might try to get unfair and improper evidence before the judge. Most of this improper evidence will have nothing to do with the issues in your case: who owes what to whom. Rather, it will be offered to try to show that you are a bad person. The fact that you might be a good person, bad person, or a good person only on Mother's Day has nothing to do with the merits of a legal claim or defense.

It does not matter at all, for example, in a suit against your neighbor for negligently spray painting the side of your house, that 10 years earlier you hit him with a knobby stick, that you don't pay your bills on time, that you get drunk every Friday night, that you never go to church, or that you have halitosis.

Because this kind of evidence does not relate to any issues in the case, it is *irrelevant*. It's unfair, and way beyond the powers of your small claims judge to decide. A higher authority must be invoked.

Similar transactions in which either party has been engaged that do not have a direct bearing on the case should be kept out. The fact that the defendant has swindled someone else in town has no bearing on the question of whether or not you have been swindled under the particular circumstances of your case.

The problem with hearsay statements has been mentioned before. These out-of-court statements, oral or written, made by someone who is not there to testify as to their truth, falsity, or completeness should be kept out of the case. There is no way to test them through cross-examination and they are not made under oath.

When a witness begins to relate what someone else told him or her, a hearsay statement is going to follow. Jump up! This is one time in your life you can ignore your mamma. Interrupt the witness by saying, "Your honor, I object. The witness is about to testify to a hearsay statement that is not admissible. It is not under oath and I cannot cross-examine that witness." The judge, who should be mindful of keeping the playing field level between the parties, will thank you in his or her heart.

Be especially wary of the other side relating that they went to a lawyer and that the lawyer told them such and such. Politely but with authority, say, "I object!" What lawyers say is often objectionable. It is also hearsay. Keep it out, along with all other specious statements your opponent will try to slip by you and into the judge's ears.

As noted before, you can object to the admission into evidence of any document that is not the original document. This rule is a variation of the one that requires all evidence to be shown to be genuine. The rule exists because one word deleted with typewriter correction fluid and retyped can change the meaning of a contract. The change may not be detected if the document that is brought to court is a copy of the changed document. Again, this is the Best Evidence Rule, and the judge may or may not enforce it strictly, depending on the degree of formality maintained in conducting the trial. If a document is not an original, and it could hurt your cause, there is no harm in objecting in order to keep it out of the judge's deliberations.

There are a few official documents that technically are hearsay, but can be admitted. For example, properly *certified* court or other certified government documents, such as motor vehicle records. The proper certification of them makes them authentic and trustworthy. Each official document originates in some government office. Someone there should have the know-how and authority to certify them as genuine. You should be able to order any certified documents you need by telephone. Sometimes prepayment for the copies and certification is required, so you may need to plan time for the mail to go both ways, or plan a trip to the particular office.

Business records can also be admitted once they are shown to be regularly kept as part of the business. This is especially helpful to a business owner plaintiff who wants to send his or her bookkeeper to testify against a defendant to recover an unpaid account. The records are considered trustworthy, because most businesspeople do not doctor their records.

For any exhibit, if the other side fails to identify the item or to show how a document came into existence, the proper objection is, "Your honor, she has failed to lay a proper foundation," or, "Your honor, she has failed to show the document/item is genuine or authentic." If the party fails to show how the exhibit relates to your case, it is *irrelevant* until such a showing is made. Each item of evidence should also be *material*; that is, it will help the judge decide the issues in the case.

Of course, any evidence that is admitted, even if you object to it, can still be shown to be untrustworthy through cross-examination. The fact that the court may look at the evidence does not destroy the other side's right to show that it is, in fact, not worthy of belief.

There are some facts that can only be proven through the opinions of *expert witnesses*: the necessity and reasonableness of medical treatment; the extent and value of damage in a car collision; psychological opinions where a party claims mental pain and suffering damage; and opinions about the results of scientific experiments and procedures, such as tests by the Textile Institute to see if your cleaner really caused that stain on your new dress.

These are matters not known to the general public, and can only be reliable if they come from people with special education, training, and experience. If your adversary, or your adversary's witness, tries to testify about any of these opinions without testimony that he or she has special qualifications that make him or her an expert, you can object that it is an opinion that can only be testified to by an expert.

Everybody has opinions, of course, and not all opinions are inadmissible. Because each of us has lived, we can show a judge that our opinions about something should be believed by showing that we have a factual basis for them through our ordinary experiences. Before you give your opinion of the value of your car, for example, you could relate that you have bought and sold several, read the want ads religiously, or were in the used car business for 10 years in your youth. Give some background, so the judge can see that your opinion is worthy of belief.

When it comes time for trial, the time for settlement is over. Your *settlement discussions* are not admissible. The other side may try to get this in to limit your recovery, if you are a plaintiff: "But Judge, he agreed to take $200 less when we were talking about this in the hall." Or this may be offered by a plaintiff to prove a right to recover: "But Judge, she agreed to pay me $200 to settle this case."

A willingness to compromise is not an issue at trial. This kind of evidence is more about your character. You do not have to settle. If you did not, to mention it might cast you in an unfair light. The inference is that you are the one creating the problem of clogged court calendars and poor overworked judges, like the one you are facing. It is not right. Keep settlement discussions out.

Sometimes the other party or witness against you will try to testify about something he or she cannot possibly know anything about. They haven't experienced it or learned about it any other way. It is unreliable because it is based totally on *speculation*. One red flag goes up is when a question begins, "Isn't it possible..." Speculation is sure to follow. Or a witness may testify that her conclusion about something is "just a guess." It is untrustworthy. Keep it out.

You know that the other side will have a chance to ask you and your witnesses questions on cross-examination. They should not be allowed to intimidate you or your witnesses through abusive questions or use an abusive manner in asking them. This may be *badgering the witness*. If it happens, object. Even if you are testifying at the time, object: "Your honor, I object to this question and this whole series of questions. They are abusive, and the manner in which they are being asked undercuts my dignity and the dignity of this court." Use your own words.

You always imagined yourself leaping to your feet and successfully making an objection, of hearing the dolorous voice of the judge intone, "Sustained." You will have your chance. It is the right thing for you to do. In each case, you are asking the judge not to consider faulty facts. Bad evidence makes for bad decisions. Nobody wants that.

5. Cross-examination. Witnesses are supposed to speak the truth. Most try, some do not. Witnesses are witnesses because they have information helpful in proving one side of a case. They have received information through their senses, processed it, and when they get to court, they describe the results of this process under oath on the stand.

The processing, accumulating, and retelling of information can be a very faulty process. All sorts of errors creep in.

If the errors hurt your case, it is your job to expose them as untruths, half-truths, partial truths, or lies. You do this by asking questions of the other party and the other party's witnesses through cross-examination. If the faulty testimony is not damaging to your side of the case, you may still try to expose it as incorrect, attacking the credibility of the opposing witness.

Before your case begins, your judge may give you instructions about questioning the witnesses for the other side. You may be told you are to ask questions, not to argue with the witness or comment on the witness's testimony. Listen to the judge with respect. Then, remember what follows.

Cross-examination is questioning people who are against you. Nice enough people, but enemies against Your Cause, which is just and true. Your goal in questioning them is to create doubt, to show that the bad things they have said about your case are clouded with uncertainty. By showing that their testimony is not worthy of belief, you undercut the strength of the opposition. You weaken it, and in the process, your case grows stronger. The scales of justice tip your way.

The more effective you are, the more likely you are to win. Every famous trial lawyer is an expert at undermining the opposition through cross-examination. Most lawyers are not good at it. They have never learned or practiced the basics. They have too much information and too little practical knowledge.

The key to undermining the other side's case by cross-examination is to *listen to what the witness says*. To actively listen requires your full attention. It requires effort and concentration. Judging looks easy. It is a great job, but listening closely for hours on end is exhausting. Studies have shown that you can expend as many calories concentrating as you do exercising. You will get tired, but it will be worth it.

There is a widely used technique to help you track a witness's testimony and highlight those points you want to attack through questioning during cross-examination. Take notes. If you divide a notebook page with a vertical line in the center from top to bottom, you can take notes in the left column while the witness is testifying and put checks or one word reminders in the right column next to each fact you want to expose as being untrustworthy. There are cross-examination pages set up this way in your Trial Notebook.

The following is offered so you will know what you are looking for. When you ask your first question, you will know what to ask. Hopefully, you will have taken notes during the witness's testimony, so you can point out where it is wrong. When you are asking questions on cross examination, listen to the responses. They may lead you to further questions.

There are three simple rules for effective cross-examination:

1. *Don't cross-examine*. If a witness hasn't hurt you, don't ask questions just for the sake of asking something.

2. *Ask questions*. Instead, make statements and turn them into questions. These can take one of two forms:

♦ "Isn't it true... (the statement follows)?"

♦ The statement followed by "wasn't it?" or "didn't you?" or a similar short phrase that changes the statement to a question. Note, too, that each of these questions requires a yes or no answer. If a witness insists, the judge will let him or her explain the answer as much as is necessary, as long as the witness is still responding to the question and not rambling off the subject. By asking questions that elicit yes or no answers, you can lead the witness along the path you want to go. Lawyers call these *leading questions*.

3. *Don't ask a question when you don't know the answer*. You will probably be surprised at the answer you get, maybe horribly surprised.

So, what do you ask? You can discredit a witness in many ways. You can attack the testimony by showing that the witness is confused, or that the whole truth is something that escaped his or her perception or reason. Very seldom will you be able to show that a witness is out and out lying. So don't worry about it, even if he or she is lying. Stick to the basics.

These are the most common areas in which you may find holes in a witness's story:

1. The witness could not know what he says he knows because he could not perceive it. Because of the circumstances at the time of the incident he is relating, he may not have been able to receive the information he says he got through his senses:

"At the time you say you saw me secretly borrow Henry's lawn mower, it was pitch black out, wasn't it?"

"Isn't it true that you were standing at least 50 yards away?"

"At the time you say you heard me shout 'Fire!' in the theater, the movie was at the part when the earthquake roars, and you really couldn't hear anything, could you?"

"At the time of the collision, you were passed out drunk in the back seat, weren't you?"

"You were looking the other way, weren't you?"

"You weren't even there when Mavis and I agreed on this contract, were you?"

"You weren't wearing your glasses, were you?"

"Isn't it true that you are legally blind?"

Other questions can be framed for the other senses, also. Note that when we experience events, we do not experience them in a vacuum. There are many things going on at once in each moment of our lives. To the extent that a person is concentrating on any one thing, his or her perception is distracted from all the rest. To the extent that he or she is taking it all in, he or she will not be likely to notice one particular thing. Either way, a witness may be unable to remember details.

"You do not remember what I was wearing the day you say I ran into your car, do you?"

"And you do not remember how many people I had in my car, do you?"

"You do not recall, do you, if the flag was flying on the flagpole that day, do you?"

"You do not recall whether you were standing six feet, 10 feet, or 12 feet away at the time, do you?"

"You couldn't tell if Mr. Bemis had one drink or five, could you?"

2. The witness cannot know what he says he knows because he does not have the education, training, or experience.

"You have never been a mechanic, have you? So, you cannot tell the difference between oil and transmission fluid by smelling it, can you?"

"You don't have any medical training, do you? So, you do not know if all the things the hospital charged me for were necessary, do you?"

"Isn't it true that the only information you have about this incident is what other people have told you about it?" (If the answer is yes, all of the witness's testimony is hearsay. You should ask the judge to disregard it and to direct the witness to leave the witness stand.)

"Isn't it true that you don't know if Ms. Johnson suffered any kind of pain at all, except by what she told you?"

"You are not in the car business, are you? So you don't really know the value of your car before the accident, do you?"

3. The testimony is suspect because the witness is biased or interested in the outcome of the case.

"The defendant is your brother, isn't he? You wouldn't do or say anything to hurt your brother, would you?"

"You work for the plaintiff, don't you? If you were to testify unfavorably against your boss, it could mean bad news for your job, couldn't it?"

"It's fair to say that you are Ms. Fetzer's best friend, isn't it? You wouldn't do anything to harm your friendship, would you?"

"Isn't it true that you are a major stockholder in the defendant's company? A judgment against the company would affect the value of your stock, wouldn't it?"

"You are the defendant's next door neighbor, aren't you? If you were to testify against your neighbor, it could affect your family for years, couldn't it?"

"You hate men, don't you?" (Substitute whatever feelings—dislike, distrust, suspicion—and whatever defining category you are in—housewives, doctors, lawyers, financial planners, contractors, painters, plumbers, performing artists, Rotary Club members, Democrats, Episcopalians, salespeople, etc.).

4. The witness's testimony is inconsistent. This can happen any of three ways. The story the witness tells can be inconsistent within itself, it can be contrary to what the witness has said at another time, and it can be inconsistent with what other witnesses have said or what the other evidence in the case shows. Again, to pick up on any of these, you need to listen to what the witness says, and mentally compare it to what you already know about the case.

To undermine the believability of the witness, all you need to do is point out the inconsistency. To repeat, take notes while the witness is testifying. Mark the places in the story where inconsistencies pop up, so you can ask the witness about them after the testimony is over.

In a case where the witness's story is not consistent from beginning to end, point it out:

"Mrs. Green, early in your testimony, you said that you were standing 20 feet away when you saw the collision. Do you remember that? Later, you said that you were 20 yards away, do you remember that? Which is it? You are not sure, are you?"

Suppose the witness has made a statement at another time that is inconsistent with the testimony at trial:

"Mr. Blue, you recall that you just testified that the light was green when you went through it, don't you? But you told me and the police officer at the wreck scene that it was yellow, didn't you?"

You can confirm this by having the witness look at the police report or by having the police officer testify what the witness said earlier, or you can testify what he said at the earlier time in order to contradict himself. This type of testimony is *rebuttal* evidence.

Note that as time passes, memories fade. So what a person said at the time of the incident that gave rise to your case, maybe three or six months ago, is more likely to be closer to the truth. (Assuming, of course, the person was trying to tell the truth then.) Also, statements made when a person doesn't have time to think are more likely to express the truth. As when the driver gets out of her car after a wreck and exclaims, "I'm so sorry. It's all my fault!"

Memories are funny. People tend to remember a version of events that causes less psychological pain to them. Eventually, they become convinced that this twisted version of the facts is true. If a witness tells a version of the story that is consistent within itself, and no amount of questioning will get him or her to change the story, the witness probably believes it is true. Your job, then, is to show that it is incorrect by other evidence—that it doesn't make sense in light of other facts that are not disputed. This is the third way to demonstrate that a witness is not telling the whole truth, and that the testimony should be disregarded or mistrusted.

Showing that testimony is not to be trusted does not mean harassing or badgering a witness. You can intimate that a person is not telling the truth, but don't call him or her a liar. A judge is likely to be offended, because it is up to the judge to decide whether a witness is telling the truth. Don't step on the judge's mental toes here. You will get a lot more leverage by treating the witness, even a boldface liar, with more respect than he or she deserves.

When you are planning your trial, you should at least have a good idea of how the other party will testify. Think about how you might be able to undermine this opposing version of things, and put it in your Trial Notebook (see page 127).

6. Choosing a Jury. In many small claims courts, you have the right to have a jury hear your case. Either you or the other side can make this choice in these courts. So it is a group of people you need to convince, instead of just one judge. No big deal. The same principles apply.

In your court, the judge may ask the prospective jurors questions to see if they know anything about your case, or are otherwise qualified to hear it.

Or the judge may let you do the choosing. This may be done by the process of elimination. After all the possible jurors have been asked questions, the parties take turns eliminating those jurors least likely to be favorable to their side. Alternately, you may question possible jurors individually until you get the necessary number, six or 12, that are not objectionable to either party. This process of asking potential jurors questions is known as *voir dire*, from the French, meaning, "To see, to say."

Do you want a jury that is fair? No! This is war. You want jurors who are most like you and least like the opposition, therefore more sympathetic to your plight. The idea is that if both parties have this strategy, an impartial jury will hear the case.

I think the most important criterion for choosing a jury in these cases is to choose people you can talk to. Then consider other factors, such as age, occupation, marital status, number of children, business expertise, or other life experiences that are similar to yours and unlike those of the other side.

The law says a juror should be totally unbiased and should come into a case with a mind free of a favorable disposition to one party or the other. Hogwash. It is the ideal, but it is never true. Everyone carries around his or her own bias baggage. If you want to win, find out what it is, and how you can use it to your advantage.

If you have a chance, talk to these people. They are just people from your community. You can find out a lot about a person by asking simple questions, such as:

"Mr. Fish, are you employed?"

"What kind of work do you do?"

"What does your job actually entail?"

"Have you always done that kind of work?"

"What do you like to do in your spare time?"

"Oh really? Have you read the book *Inner Golf?*"

"What books have you read in the last six months?"

"Do you watch golf on TV?"

"What else do you like to watch?"

"Do you know my opponent or any of his witnesses?"

Get very interested in these people for a short time. You can see that the answers to any one of these questions could lead you to a place where you are on common ground with the juror, that you have shared experience, that you are alike, and that Mr. Fish should feel as you do about your cause and rule in your favor.

Once the jury is chosen, your case will be tried the same as if a judge was hearing the case alone. While the judge will still control what exhibits and testimony is trustworthy enough to be considered by the jury, the jurors will decide who wins and how much. So talk to them when testifying and have your witnesses do the same. When you have an exhibit that the judge has said is admissible, show it to the jury. If you have documents that are important to your case, make enough copies so the jury can follow along. Get them involved in your case.

If the evidence is equal on both sides, you will be more likely to win if the jury likes you better. It may not seem fair, but that's reality.

7. Closing Statement. This is your final destination, the last thing you do before the judge pronounces the judgment. The closing statement is a summary of what you think the evidence in the case has shown—that you are entitled to win. Highlight your strong points, and downplay your weak points and the opposition's strong points. Be brief, convincing, and say "thank you" to the judge or jury at the end.

Don't feel bad if the judge does not allow you to make a closing statement. She may feel that the evidence is clear so that no further explanation of it is necessary. It is not a slight against you or your case. You are done. Relax. It's up to someone else now. Kind of scary, isn't it?

8. What If You Lose? It's possible (but unlikely if you have done your job)—even the best trial lawyers sometimes lose cases. In every case, someone must lose. It may be your turn. A judgment is just the official opinion as to who should win and how much. Like all opinions, they can be wrong, and can be changed.

All is not lost! You can appeal, and the good news is, that most of the appeals from small claims court get you a whole new trial, from beginning to end. Before you leave, check with the clerk to find out, if you have not already done so. You will want to know how long you have to appeal, what court you will appeal to, whether the clerk's office provides the forms, and the cost, if any.

If you accept the judgment but cannot pay it in full, ask the judge to set up a payment schedule. Many courts allow it. Or you could ask the winning party directly to accept a payment schedule. (See the Judgment Payment Agreement form in Chapter 24.)

Leave the courthouse. Get some perspective. If your resolve is strengthened by your trial experience and your further contemplation of the situation, go for it. File your appeal.

9. When You Win. Smile wide and deep. Congratulate yourself to the point of embarrassment. Now, back to earth. What you have won is a *judgment*, the right to get money or property from the losing party sufficient to satisfy your claim. This is done in different ways in different courts.

The best and quickest way is to ask the loser, still with respect for being a worthy adversary, "When might I expect to be paid?" Agree to accept payments. While a judgment gives you the right to go about looking for the defeated's property for seizure and sale to satisfy you, you may be able to get paid in full without having to go to this trouble. The Judgment Payment Agreement in Chapter 24 is good for both situations.

Once your judgment is entered, you will be entitled to interest on it at the rate established by law in your state.

If your offer to accept payments is turned down before you leave the courtroom and the courthouse, ask the judge or clerk, "How do I collect?" If there is information available, you will have it in hand when you leave. Strategies for collection are explained in Chapter 22. One caution: It may be risky to start seizing the other side's money or property before the time for appeal has run. Check with the clerk about this interval, and ask what is normally done in your court.

Chapter 21

Your Trial Notebook

Plaintiffs, remember, you need to prove two things to the satisfaction of the judge: that you have a right to recover, and how much. Defendants, you need to show only that the plaintiff is not so entitled. If you are a defendant with a counterclaim, act like a plaintiff with it: prove that you are entitled to win on your counterclaim and how much.

Last winning tactic: When filling in your notebook, complete your closing statement first. It is where you are going with all of this. Doing it first will focus your effort.

I. Opening statement. Plaintiffs: "Your honor, my name is _____, and this case involves a _____ (contract or tort) and I am claiming damages in the amount of $_____."

"I expect the evidence will show (outline the high points of your case in one or two paragraphs) _____

_____

_____

_____

_____

_____

_____

Defendants: "On the contrary, the evidence will show _____
_____
_____

(summary of your case).

II. Testimony of first witness or yourself.

    A. Facts to be shown _____
_____
_____
_____
_____

    B. Documents or other exhibits to be identified and introduced by this witness and facts to be shown by each:

        1. Exhibit 1. _____
_____
_____

        2. Exhibit 2. _____
_____
_____

III. Second witness.

    A. Facts to be shown _____
_____
_____
_____

    B. Documents or other exhibits to be identified and introduced by this witness and facts to shown by each:

        1. Exhibit 3. _____
_____
_____

        2. Exhibit 4. _____
_____
_____

IV. Third witness.

A. Facts to be shown _____

_____

_____

_____

B. Documents or other exhibits to be identified and introduced by this witness and facts to shown by each:

    1. Exhibit 5. _____

_____

_____

    2. Exhibit 6. _____

_____

_____

V. Objections. While the other side is cross-examining your witnesses, you can object if they *badger* or intimidate your witnesses, or even if they are rude: "Your honor, I object that the other side is treating my witness this way. In court, I expect to treat everyone with dignity and respect, and I expect other people to do it, too."

VI. Have your exhibits admitted into evidence. *Very important!!* If you haven't done it along the way, put all of your exhibits in evidence. That is, make sure the judge will consider them when making the decision. Say something like, "Judge, I would like to enter Exhibits 1 through _____ at this time."

VII. Objections to testimony and exhibits offered by the other side. For each of these you have a reason to oppose, stand and say, "Your honor, I object." Then tell why:

A. This testimony/exhibit is *irrelevant*. It doesn't have anything to do with the issues in this case.

B. This testimony is *hearsay*. Or, the statements in this documents are hearsay. The statements were made out of court by someone who is not here to testify. They are not under oath, and I cannot test them by cross-examination. They are inherently unreliable and untrustworthy.

C. This exhibit should not be considered as part of this case, because the other party has not shown its connection to this case. There has been *no foundation laid* for it to be considered.

D. The question calls for an *opinion* of the witness, and it has not been shown that the witness has any background to make such an opinion.

E. The question calls for an answer that can only be provided by *expert opinion*. This witness has not been shown to be an expert.

VIII. Cross-examination. You point out that the witness may not be believed by asking them questions showing:

1. *Their perception was bad.* The circumstances were such that they couldn't record the events accurately through their senses.

2. *They are biased.* The witness is so linked with the other party, their testimony is suspicious.

3. *The testimony doesn't make sense.*

    a) It is not consistent from beginning to end.

    b) It is not consistent with other evidence.

    c) It is not consistent with statements made by the witness at another time.

4. *The witness's memory is bad.* He or she cannot remember details.

Cross Examination Pages

As mentioned before, one widely used technique to highlight the points you want to attack on cross-examination involves taking notes on one side of a piece of paper and checking or marking next to your notes what you want to ask a question about. This is set up for you on the following pages. If you know the particular questions you want to ask, you can note these while you are planning.

Example:

Testimony	**Point**
_____	_____
_____	_____
_____	_____

IX. Rebuttal. Plaintiffs, if a counterclaim has been prosecuted against you, you should have a chance to prove your case against it.

A. First Rebuttal Witness _____

    Facts: _____

    _____

    _____

B. Second Rebuttal Witness _____

    Facts: _____

    _____

    _____

Testimony	Point
_____	_____
_____	_____
_____	_____
_____	_____
_____	_____
_____	_____
_____	_____
_____	_____
_____	_____
_____	_____
_____	_____
_____	_____
_____	_____
_____	_____
_____	_____
_____	_____
_____	_____
_____	_____
_____	_____
_____	_____
_____	_____

Testimony	Point
_____	_____
_____	_____
_____	_____
_____	_____
_____	_____
_____	_____
_____	_____
_____	_____
_____	_____
_____	_____
_____	_____
_____	_____
_____	_____
_____	_____
_____	_____
_____	_____
_____	_____
_____	_____
_____	_____
_____	_____

X. Closing statement. Summarize in up to five minutes everything that has been positive about your case and negative about the other side's. Point out any evidence that has not been refuted. Finish by telling the judge exactly what you want him or her to do. Plaintiffs: "When you consider all the evidence, you will see that I have proven that I am entitled to a judgment in the amount of $_____ and my court costs." Defendants: "When you consider all the evidence, you can see that the plaintiff is not entitled to recover anything, and (if applicable) I am entitled to recover a judgment on my counterclaim in the amount of $_____."

_____

_____

_____

_____

_____

_____

_____

_____

_____

XI. Choosing a jury. Establish brief friendships. Eliminate those likely to be sympathetic to your opponent's point of view. Talk to them. Choose those you can talk to. Check for obvious bias. Expose any strongly held opinions about the subjects of your case. If it involves a dog bite, see if you have animal lovers; if it is about the wrongful cutting of trees, look for environmentalists; if it is an auto repair case against a dealer, find out if anybody works for a dealership, is a mechanic, or is related to one.

    A. Background questions.

        Age: _____

        Marital status: _____

        Children: (If grown, ask what they do.) _____

        _____

        Employment: (If you find out exactly what their job is, you will find that they will talk to you more easily.) _____

        Hobbies, interests, books read, movies seen:_____

        _____

        _____

    B. Legal experience.

        Prior jury experience: _____

        Any cases like yours? _____

(Note: Prior jury experience can be positive or negative. Note how they react when you ask them these questions.)

Prior legal training? _____

C. Orientation to this case.

Know the other party or any of their witnesses? _____

Know anything about this case? _____

D. Cleanup.

"Is there reason at all that any of you do not want to sit on this jury?"

_____

_____

"Are there any of you who think you could not give a fair verdict after hearing all the evidence?" _____

_____

PART V

Nice Work, Nice Judgment. What Now?

CHAPTER 22

COLLECTING YOUR JUDGMENT

You are warm with the glow of victory, but begin to notice that your pocket is still empty. Well, you do have that piece of paper you got from the judge saying that you won. But what is it exactly that you have won? And how do you move money from the loser's pocket into yours?

The judgment says to the world that you have a right to find the loser's property and turn it into enough cash to satisfy the claim you have proven. You and the loser have formal legal names: You are the *judgment creditor* and the defeated is your *judgment debtor*. What you have is a *judgment lien*.

When a judgment is signed and filed in the clerk's office, it binds all of the judgment debtor's property—real estate, personal property, and cash. It is like a padlock secured to the debtor's property. It cannot be removed until you get paid.

What is even better, your judgment binds all of the property he or she gets later, until your judgment is fully satisfied. Even "more better," you are entitled to collect interest on the unpaid balance until you are paid. The judgment debtor has what the court has said is your money. For heavens sake, go get it!

Ordinarily the court will not get the money for you. But in some courts, they do. Check with the clerk.

The clerk might help by placing your judgment on a court record so that all the world will know of your right to recover. This serves as notice to all that your padlock is locked firmly in place. The clerk should issue a document known as an *execution*. The execution directs any officer having the authority to seize and sell property to satisfy judgments, to go ahead and do it for you. By filing the execution in any county or city where your judgment debtor has property, the seizing officers there will have the same authority to help you get your money.

"Whoopee," you say. Despite your first reaction, this can be valuable when the judgment debtor tries to sell real estate or get credit. In order to get good title to real estate, a buyer will require that all judgments be paid before the seller gets paid. So, you get yours first. Of course, it may be some time before the loser decides to sell his or her real estate. Patience. As mentioned before, when you receive a judgment, you also receive the right to collect interest on it at the legal rate in your state. If it does not state on your judgment or execution something like, "with interest at the legal rate until paid," call the clerk again.

One caution: Although your right to collect on your judgment stays viable for a number of years, some day it will expire. You should try to collect as quickly as you can. Joyfully, you can use any or all of the collection methods at your disposal at the same time until you are satisfied and have recovered all your money, including the interest.

Collection is a two-step procedure: You find the judgment debtor's property, then convert it to cash to satisfy your judgment.

Finding the debtor's property can be fun and interesting. You can be your own detective or hire a service to do an assets search for you for a fee. Your local credit reporting service is a good place to start. If they do not offer this search service, they will know who does in your area.

You may already know much of what the debtor owns through your earlier dealings. Did he or she ever give you a check? It was issued from an account in a bank or credit union somewhere that is bound to have more money where the first came from. Does your debtor drive a car? Has he ever mentioned a super-duper speedboat, airplane, home theater system, favorite chair, horse, or dog? You can target any and all of the property your debtor has and all he or she is entitled to from other people—his or her employer, anyone who owes him or her money, and the business receivables of any business he or she has an interest in.

Courthouse records are a rich source of information on who owns what. Real estate records index landowners alphabetically. Tax records sometimes show substantial personal property, business property, boats, and motor vehicles in the county or city that collects a tax on them.

You may be able to find what motor vehicles the judgment debtor owns by contacting your state motor vehicles bureau. While you are talking with them, find out if your state has a procedure that allows you to place a lien on the front of a judgment debtor's motor vehicle.

State taxing authorities may also have records of personal property having a substantial value, over $1,000 for example, so the state can tax it. You can drive by the debtor's house to see what is in the driveway and yard. But don't look in the windows. You could be subject to a suit for invasion of privacy or arrested as a "Peeping Tom."

In many courts, you can simply ask the loser. These courts allow *post-judgment discovery*, the purpose being to discover what property the judgment debtor has to satisfy the judgment. The clerk may provide you with a form with a series of questions, formally called *interrogatories*, asking the location and value of real estate and personal property—vehicles, bank accounts, employment, and the like. The judgment debtor is required in a limited time to answer the questions fully, usually under oath, then to file the answers with the clerk and send you a copy. These interrogatories can be enforced like a subpoena to the extent that if the debtor is stubborn in refusing to answer, he or she may end up in jail. Refusing to answer may result in a finding of contempt by the debtor against the issuing court.

You may not be alone in your search for property to seize and sell. Your debtor may have other people who have established their claims by judgment before you did, so there may be other judgment padlocks on the property. These competing claims can make the collection process a little complicated. In most states, the rule of, "first in time, first in line," applies. This simply means that the first person to establish a claim against the property of another has the first chance to have it sold to satisfy the claim.

Collecting your judgment when there are others is only dangerous when the debtor has signed a security agreement or mortgage and the other creditors have a *secured interest* in the property. Cars, rent-to-own appliances, business equipment, business furniture, and home furnishings are common subjects of security interests. Security interests are created when someone wants to buy any of these items on credit. The seller/merchant and buyer agree that in exchange for the buyer's promise to make monthly payments, the buyer can have the property before it is paid for. The seller agrees to this as long as the property is pledged on paper as security for the debt. If the buyer fails to make the payments, the seller has the right to repossess the goods and sue for the balance owed on the debt. As part of the transaction, the buyer will sign a Uniform Commercial Code Financing Statement, an FS-1 form, describing the property and the debt. The buyer records this on the public records at the courthouse so that anyone who wants to know can find out that the merchant has a claim on the property and a right to repossess it.

This same arrangement exists for the purchase of most motor vehicles in this country, except that the seller's lien is recorded on the title of the motor vehicle. Once you have your judgment lien placed on the title, as in the case of real estate, it will be practically impossible for the owner to sell it without paying off your judgment.

The danger in seizing and selling property subject to a security interest lies in the fact that the secured lender has a right to have his or her debt paid off first. If you seize and sell the property, you can be subject to a lawsuit for dealing wrongfully with this secured property interest, and the money you realize from the sale may be taken by the secured creditor.

To avoid this, you can check the courthouse records to see if the clerk has judgment, mortgage, or security interest liens indexed there. These indexes may be kept in a clerk's office in a court other than the small claims court, but the clerk of the small claims court will know where you can find them. These indexes are usually alphabetical by the last name of the debtor, or by the first letter in the name of a debtor corporation. A *general execution docket* will contain all the judgments against a person or a business in the county or court district. You will find financing statements, those FS-1 forms, in an index variously called the *business docket, commercial docket,* or *UCC* (for Uniform Commercial Code) *docket.*

Once you find out what property is available and where it is, there are two chief methods available to you to collect your judgment:

1. Levy and Sale. Once you find property that is free of liens or security interests, tell the officer in your city or county with the authority to seize and sell it to go ahead. This will be a county or city sheriff, constable, or marshal. You will need to describe for the officer the property to be seized and the location. The levying officer may have a truck and men to load and carry off the property or you may need to arrange for a truck and loaders. Once you learn who the appropriate levying officer is, ask what you need to do. If the levying officer will only stand by while you load the property, you can bring your friends or hire a moving company to help you.

These officers can "seize" real estate by notifying the owner that the levy has taken place, and by advertising a public sale in the local newspaper that carries the legal ads.

Any property seized by levy is sold at the next sheriff's sale or sale held periodically by the levying officer for this purpose. You get the money after the expenses of the sale are paid. Because this property is being sold at a forced sale, the property sold does not often bring its fair market value. Knowing this, the judgment debtor may come to the sale and bid low to get his or her property back. If this happens, once the levying officer has the cash, if it is not sufficient to pay your whole judgment, immediately ask the officer to levy on it again so it can be sold at the next sale. You won't even have to move it.

2. Garnishment. A garnishment is a special lawsuit against someone who owes the judgment debtor money, or who holds his or her money, chiefly his or her employer or banker. If the defendant in this suit, the *garnishee*, has the debtor's money, he or she is required to pay it into court so the clerk can pay it out to you. Any costs of the garnishment action are collected with the money collected by the garnishment itself. Where this remedy is available, it is commonly used because it is very simple. The clerk of the local court, which may be the small claims court you sued in or another court, should provide you with all the forms. My experience has been that the forms provided have extensive instructions and other information describing exactly how the garnishment procedure works in that court.

The garnishment for wages differs from the bank garnishment only in that you would have the right to have the employer pay over a portion of the debtor's wages for a set number of weeks, usually more than six. If you have not been fully satisfied by then, you can file another garnishment against the same employer, recover the balance of your money, plus the additional costs in connection with the second garnishment. Employers are most often prohibited from firing their employees while their wages are being garnished. Everybody is happy. You get your money, the debtor keeps his or her job, and once again, the system works.

Caution: Bankruptcy!

If you learn that your judgment debtor has filed, or might have filed, an action in United States Bankruptcy Court, *stop!* At the time of filing, a bar raises against all those seeking to recover or who have any claim on the property of the filer. If you continue to pursue your judgment once the bankruptcy has been filed, you can be subject to a finding of contempt by a judge in the bankruptcy court and jailed. Bankruptcy judges are serious about this, and although you might not be jailed, your life can be interrupted by your being summoned to court to stop you from carrying on your collection efforts.

The purpose of bankruptcy is to protect honest debtors from their creditors long enough for them to get back on their financial feet. A filing under Chapter Seven of the Bankruptcy Code asks the bankruptcy judge to cancel all the debts that are listed. A filing under Chapter 13 includes a payment plan so that the debtor can pay off his or her debts wholly or partially over time.

You should be notified by mail that a Petition in Bankruptcy has been filed by the clerk of the bankruptcy court. The notice will contain the case number and the dates of any hearings that have been scheduled. If you get one, call the clerk—the telephone number is somewhere on the form—and ask if you need to appear at the hearings.

You may not be formally notified. You might only hear a rumor that your debtor has filed for bankruptcy. These laws are so strong for the debtor, that you have a duty to inquire about it by calling the clerk. The number is in the white pages of the phone book.

Once you know, you are *absolutely prohibited* from trying to collect on your judgment without permission of the bankruptcy judge until the bankruptcy case is dismissed or ends. If your claim is forgiven or *discharged* in a Chapter Seven case, you are forever barred from getting your money.

And then? Consider the value of all you have learned in the process. Go live, learn, and enjoy some more.

CHAPTER 23

THE END

But wait! There are no endings without beginnings. That is why there are so many movie sequels. When the civil justice system described here works well, it is an extraordinary example of human ingenuity. Despite its detractors, no other system offers to so many easy access to a means for righting wrongs without violence.

Those who work in the legal profession, who take the law seriously yet delight in its intricacies, give it its unique dignity. As said before, most are in that line of work because they believe they can make a positive difference in society. Every day, our legal system reinforces the notion that every individual stands equal before the law. It is societal glue.

Each litigant, whether the claim is for $10 or a $1 million, can rely on his or her rights being adjusted in conformity with all others who have similarly stood in a court asking for relief.

This civil justice system speaks volumes to the world about the value our society places on the rights of each individual. To each person, especially one who would pursue or defend his own case, it gives a handle on history. Each case tried becomes a bit of experience to guide future litigants. It joins the now millions who have contributed to a tradition going back hundreds of years here and hundreds more in Europe.

What has been offered here is given to suggest that in enforcing your own legal rights, there are no problems, only challenges. You create your own adventure by taking the challenges offered to you; you grow, and become more alive in the process. When you learn, you are better.

Ah, it's fun to try. Enjoy yourself. You have the tools. Go for it.

CHAPTER 24

FORMS

These forms are meant to show what you would expect in those provided by the clerk of your local court. The settlement forms are less likely to be the same as those your clerk might provide, but are adaptable to most situations.

They are in the order you expect to use them through pre-trial, trial, and post-judgment stages.

A. Complaint/Statement of Claim: May also be called a Petition for Relief. The document filed to start a lawsuit.

B. Summons: Attached to and served with the Complaint. Officially notifies the defendant that he or she has been sued.

C. Answer and Counterclaim: After a summons has been served, the defendant must file an Answer in a time limited by local rule. The Counterclaim sets forth the basis of any counter-suit the defendant may have against the plaintiff. The Complaint, Answer and Counterclaim define the issues involved in the trial.

D. Third Party Complaint/Statement of Claim: Filed by the defendant who claims the third party is liable for part or all the damages the defendant may owe to the plaintiff, if any. The defendant is then known as the *Third Party Plaintiff,* and the third party, the *Third Party Defendant,* because that is their procedural relation.

E. Consent Order: To settle a case after filing and before trial. Approved by the judge and filed with the clerk.

F. Dismissal After Consent Order: Notifies the clerk that the terms of your consent order have been completed. The plaintiff can file a simpler form of this any time the case settles, or when he or she no longer wants to pursue it. If there is a counterclaim in the case, the case will not be dismissed, but the defendant's claim will proceed against the plaintiff.

G. Affidavit for Entry of a Default Judgment: Filed by the plaintiff when the defendant fails to file an Answer in time. May contain attachments showing specifically how much you claim you are entitled to in the judgment.

H. Consent Judgment: The defendant agrees that the plaintiff should win, and agrees to have judgment entered against him or her.

I. Consent Judgment/Payment Agreement: The defendant agrees the plaintiff wins. The plaintiff agrees to take installments until the defendant fails to make one on time. If the defendant misses, the plaintiff is entitled to a judgment for the unpaid balance.

J. Judgment Payment Agreement: After judgment has been entered, the plaintiff agrees to take installments until the defendant fails to make one on time. If the defendant misses, the plaintiff is entitled to a judgment for the unpaid balance.

K. Affidavit and Notice of Default: filed by the plaintiff to notify the court that the defendant has failed to live up to any of the above agreements, asking for the unpaid balance.

Note: In all cases where the form involves some agreement between the parties where payment is involved, "Plaintiff" and "Defendant" are interchangeable. For example, in form I, the plaintiff, having lost on a counterclaim at trial, may be required to make payments to the defendant.

FORM A

FILED: _____ CIVIL ACTION NO. _____

IN THE _____ COURT OF _____

STATE OF _____

PLAINTIFF _____   *   DEFENDANT _____

Address_____   *   Address_____

_____   *   _____

_____   VS.   _____

COMPLAINT/STATEMENT OF CLAIM

_____ Contract   _____ Tort   _____ Account   _____ Other: _____

1. This Court has jurisdiction in this case.

2. Plaintiff is entitled to have a judgment against Defendant because (explain):

_____

_____

_____

_____

3. The claim is in the amount of $_____, calculated as follows: _____

_____

_____

and all costs of this suit.

_____
PLAINTIFF

SWORN TO and Subscribed before me

This _____ day of _____, _____.

_____
Clerk/Notary Public

FORM B

FILED: _____ CIVIL ACTION NO. _____

IN THE _____ COURT OF _____

STATE OF _____

PLAINTIFF _____   *   DEFENDANT _____

Address_____   *   Address_____

_____   *   _____

_____   VS.   _____

SUMMONS

TO THE ABOVE NAMED DEFENDANT:

      YOU ARE HEREBY SUMMONED and required to file an Answer with the Clerk of this Court, and serve the Plaintiff with a copy of it by regular mail to Plaintiff at the above address **within ___ days of service** of this Summons upon you.

      If you fail to do so, judgment for the full amount asked for by the Plaintiff in the Complaint/Statement of Claim will be entered against you by default.

      This ____ day of _____, _____.

_____
CLERK / DEPUTY CLERK OF COURT

TO DEFENDANT: This copy was **served** upon you

This ____ day of _____, _____.

_____
Agent for Service of Process

FORM C

CIVIL ACTION NO. _____

IN THE _____ COURT OF _____

STATE OF _____

PLAINTIFF _____ * DEFENDANT _____

Address_____ * Address_____

_____ * _____

_____ <u>VS.</u> _____

ANSWER

___ I am not indebted to Plaintiff in any amount.

___ I am indebted to Plaintiff in a different amount: $_____.

___ I am indebted to Plaintiff, but Plaintiff owes me more.

Answering further: (explain)_____

_____

COUNTERCLAIM

1. This court has jurisdiction because of the Complaint.

2. Defendant is entitled to have a judgment against Plaintiff because (explain):

_____

_____

3. The counterclaim is in the amount of $_____, calculated as follows:

_____

_____

_____
DEFENDANT

SWORN TO and Subscribed before me

This ____ day of _____, _____.

_____
Clerk/Notary Public

FORM D

CIVIL ACTION NO. _____

IN THE _____ COURT OF _____

STATE OF _____

PLAINTIFF _____ * DEFENDANT _____

Address _____ * Address _____

_____ * _____

_____ VS. _____

VS. _____

THIRD PARTY DEFENDANT _____

Address _____

THIRD PARTY COMPLAINT/STATEMENT OF CLAIM

Defendant makes this claim against the Third Party Defendant as follows:

1. To whatever extent Defendant is liable to Plaintiff on the claims stated in the

Complaint/Statement of Claim in this case, the Third Party Defendant is indebted to this

Defendant/Third Party Plaintiff because:

_____

_____

_____

2. Third Party Defendant is liable to Third Party Plaintiff:

    A) In any amount Defendant may be liable to Plaintiff; or

    B) The amount of $_____, calculated as follows: _____

_____,

and all costs of this suit.

    This _____ day of _____, _____.

_____
DEFENDANT/THIRD PARTY PLAINTIFF

CERTIFICATE OF SERVICE

THIS IS TO CERTIFY that I have mailed the Plaintiff a copy of the above Third Party Complaint/Statement of Claim by depositing it in the United States Mail postage prepaid and properly addressed to the Plaintiff at Plaintiff's address stated above.

This _____ day of _____, _____.

_____
DEFENDANT/THIRD PARTY PLAINTIFF

Note: Although you may not be required to send the Third Party Defendant a copy of this, because he will be served just as if he were sued originally, you should wait a few days after filing, and mail a copy certified mail to assure it is received.

FORM E

IN THE _____ COURT OF _____

STATE OF _____

_____
Plaintiff

vs.

_____
Defendant

*
*
*   CIVIL ACTION
*   FILE NO. _____

CONSENT ORDER

       THE PARTIES IN THIS CASE HAVING AGREED, Defendant shall pay to the Plaintiff $_____, payable at the rate of $_____ weekly/biweekly/monthly, the first payment being due on _____, _____, and each subsequent payment due weekly/biweekly/monthly thereafter.

       Plaintiff will take no action to seek judgment as long as payments are made on schedule. If any payment is more than three days late, upon written notice to this Court, Plaintiff shall have a judgment for the full amount left remaining. If paid in full according to schedule, Plaintiff shall dismiss this action within 5 days of receiving the last payment.

All payments shall be sent to:

_____

_____

     This _____ day of _____, _____.

_____
JUDGE

CONSENTED TO:

_____   _____
PLAINTIFF   DEFENDANT

Note on use of form: Use when you agree and where no judgment is to be entered.

FORM F

IN THE _____ COURT OF _____

STATE OF _____

_____   *
Plaintiff   *

vs.   *   CIVIL ACTION

_____   *   FILE NO. _____
Defendant   *

DISMISSAL AFTER CONSENT ORDER

THE PARTIES IN THIS CASE HAVING entered into a Consent Order on (date)

_____, _____, _____, and the agreement having been fully performed, the parties

hereby dismiss any and all claims they have filed in this case.

This _____ day of _____, _____.

_____   _____
PLAINTIFF   DEFENDANT

Note on use of form: This is used to notify the clerk that everything between the parties has been re-solved. This will close the court's file in this case.

FORM G

IN THE _____ COURT OF _____

STATE OF _____

_____	*
Plaintiff	*
vs.	* CIVIL ACTION
_____	* FILE NO. _____
Defendant	

AFFIDAVIT FOR ENTRY OF DEFAULT JUDGMENT

BEFORE ME, the undersigned duly authorized attesting officer, _____,

who says under oath:

1. I am the Plaintiff in the above case.

2. The Complaint/Statement of Claim was properly served on the Defendant, _____,

on (date) _____ __, _____, _____.

3. The Defendant has not filed an Answer nor other response to the suit in the time allowed by

law.

4. Plaintiff is entitled to a default judgment in the full amount asked for in the Complaint/

Statement of Claim, plus court costs.

_____

PLAINTIFF

Sworn to and subscribed before me

This _____ day of _____, _____.

_____

Notary Public (Seal)

Note on use of form: To be signed and filed by Plaintiff on the day after the last day and Answer was
due.

FORM H

IN THE _____ COURT OF _____

STATE OF _____

_____	*
Plaintiff	*
vs.	* CIVIL ACTION
_____	* FILE NO. _____
Defendant	*

CONSENT JUDGMENT

THE PARTIES HAVING AGREED THAT A JUDGMENT BE ENTERED IN THIS

CASE.

It is hereby <u>ORDERED:</u>

Plaintiff shall have a judgment against Defendant in the amount of $_____ plus

Court Costs of $_____, plus post-judgment interest at the rate of ____% per year until paid.

This _____ day of _____, _____.

_____
JUDGE

CONSENTED TO:

_____   _____
PLAINTIFF   DEFENDANT

Note on use of form: Use when you agree that a judgment is due, and Defendant is not in a position to make payments. Once entered, Plaintiff can start the collection process.

Winning in Small Claims Court

FORM I

IN THE _____ COURT OF _____

STATE OF _____

_____
Plaintiff

vs.

_____
Defendant

* * * *

CIVIL ACTION

FILE NO. _____

CONSENT JUDGMENT/PAYMENT AGREEMENT

THE PARTIES IN THIS CASE HAVING AGREED THAT A JUDGMENT BE ENTERED IN THIS CASE, it is hereby ORDERED: Plaintiff shall have a judgment against Defendant in the amount of $_____ plus Court Costs of $_____. Defendant shall be allowed to make payments to Plaintiff at the rate of $_____ weekly/ biweekly/monthly, beginning (date) _____, _____, _____, and each subsequent payment due weekly/biweekly/monthly thereafter.

Plaintiff will take no action to enforce this judgment as long as payments are made on schedule. If any payment is more than three days late, Plaintiff shall have all right to enforce the judgment for the full amount left remaining.

All payments shall be sent to: _____

This _____ day of _____, _____.

_____
JUDGE

CONSENTED TO:

_____ _____
PLAINTIFF   DEFENDANT

Note on use of form: Use when you agree and where judgment is to be entered. This is to the Plaintiff's advantage, because the judgment is established, and to the Defendant's because no action to collect will be taken as long as payments are current.

FORM J

IN THE _____ COURT OF _____

STATE OF _____

_____
Plaintiff

vs.

_____
Defendant

*
*
*   CIVIL ACTION
*   FILE NO. _____

JUDGMENT PAYMENT AGREEMENT

A JUDGMENT HAVING BEEN ENTERED IN THIS CASE IN THE AMOUNT OF

$_____, it is hereby <u>AGREED BETWEEN THE PARTIES:</u>   Defendant shall be allowed

to make payments to Plaintiff at the rate of $_____ weekly/ biweekly/monthly, beginning

_____, ___, _____, and each subsequent payment due weekly/biweekly/monthly thereafter.

Plaintiff will take no action to enforce this judgment as long as payments are made on

schedule. If any payment is more than three days late, Plaintiff shall have all right to enforce the

judgment for the full amount left remaining, plus any costs attendant to collection.

All payments shall be sent to: _____

This _____ day of _____, _____.

CONSENTED TO:

_____
PLAINTIFF

_____
DEFENDANT

Note on use of form: It is not necessary to file this with the Clerk, but the Defendant should file it. Because the judgment has already been entered, the Plaintiff will be able to take no action to collect as long as payments are current.

FORM K

IN THE _____ COURT OF _____

STATE OF _____

_____	*
Plaintiff	*
	* CIVIL ACTION
vs.	*
	* FILE NO. _____
_____	
Defendant	

AFFIDAVIT AND NOTICE OF DEFAULT

BEFORE ME, the undersigned duly authorized attesting officer, _____,

who says under oath:

1. I am the Plaintiff in the above case.

2. The parties entered into a (**Consent Order**) (**Consent Judgment/Payment Agreement**)

(**Judgment Payment Agreement**) on (date) _____, _____, _____.

3. Defendant has defaulted in the agreed upon payments and there is a balance due the Plaintiff

in the amount of $_____.

4. Plaintiff is entitled to a judgment and execution in this amount, plus interest at the legal rate

from the date of the entry of the Final Judgment in this case.

_____
PLAINTIFF

Sworn to and subscribed before me

This _____ day of _____, _____.

_____
Notary Public (Seal)

Note on use of form: Use when the payments have not been made under any of the listed agreements. When filed, ask the clerk the timing and procedure so that you can start collection as soon as possible.

PART VI

Appendices

Appendix 1

Questions to Ask the Clerk

This list is not meant to be exhaustive, only suggestive. The best friend you can have when going to court for the first time is a court clerk. The information you get is likely to be based on experience with hundreds of cases over many years. Pay this person a lot of respect, and you will have a mentor—someone who will guide you through your first venture.

Though highly knowledgeable, clerks are likely to be harried and sure to be grossly underpaid. They deal with an often rude and ignorant public every day. Be the exception. Be courteous and prepared. Show you respect the court clerk and his or her time. The clerk may be delightfully surprised to hear a pleasant, intelligent voice at the other end of the phone, or to see such a person standing in the office, and you will be rewarded far beyond your effort.

Here are 12 very useful questions to ask. No doubt you will come up with other good ones on your own, depending on the specifics of your case.

1. "What is the top dollar amount of the cases that are heard in your court?"

2. "My suit involves _____ (a one-sentence summary of your case.) Is this the kind of case that is heard in your court?"

3. "If I have a claim for more, can I still sue in your court if I agree to accept only the top dollar amount you handle if I win?"

4. "My claim is for $_____. Can I get additional damages because of the kind of claim I have?"

5. (If you are seeking the return of your property) "I am suing because I want my
_____ back. If I win, can your judge order it to be returned to me,
or will I only get a money judgment?"

6. "Whom do I call (and what is the telephone number, if you have it) to find out if
the business I want to sue is incorporated?"

7. "The defendant lives in _____ (city/county); or, the business I am
suing has an office or store in _____ (city/county). Can I sue in your
court?"

8. "Does your court require a settlement procedure before trial? Is one available?
How does it work?"

9. "When I come to file my suit, what do I need to bring with me? How much does it
cost? How much if I sue more than one person?"

10. "How do I get subpoenas? Who serves them? What happens if a witness I
subpoena doesn't come to court?"

11. "Do you know whom I can call or where I can go to get further information about
my kind of case?" or "Do you know any lawyers who might talk to me for a couple
of minutes about my case without charging a whole lot?"

12. "Do you have any printed information about how to sue or defend a case in your
court? How can I get a copy?"

More Definitions

Accident. When an event occurs and no one is at fault. A defense to a claim of intentional or negligent tort.

Affidavit. A written statement under oath before an officer authorized to administer oaths, such as a notary public.

Agent. Someone who has authority to act for another. Could be a person or a company. One who wrongs you while acting for another with authority for the other, binds the other. So, if your hardware store clerk, while showing you a 16-lb. sledge hammer, drops it and smashes your toe, the hardware store owner may be liable for the injury along with the clerk. Agents contract for their bosses, too.

Breach of Contract. Violation of the terms of an agreement.

Burden of Proof. The requirement placed on a party asserting a fact to prove it.

Calendar. A printed schedule of cases to be heard on any court day.

Character Evidence. Testimony or other evidence tending to show that someone is a bad person or a good person. Usually not admissible at trial because it doesn't matter. It is irrelevant.

Collateral. Property held as security to assure the payment of an obligation. The lender then has a **security interest** in the pledged property.

Contract. An agreement between two or more parties for the doing or not doing of something specified. See Chapter 8.

Contributory Negligence. When the lack of care on the part of the person injured is greater than that of the person causing the injury, the injured person loses.

Corporation. A fictional person created by the law; a legal entity, authorized by state law, which acts through the people who constitute it. These persons usually cannot be held liable personally for what they do while acting for the corporation.

Defamation. Untruthfully attacking the good name of another's personal or business reputation. *Slander* is oral; *libel* is written. Truth is the best defense.

Defense of Others. A person is justified in using such force as is reasonably necessary to protect others from assault.

Discovery. The process of finding out what the opposite side is relying on in opposing you in a law suit. After an Answer is filed, and before trial, procedural rules may allow parties to send to each other and to witnesses, written questions, requests to produce documents, or requests to admit certain facts.

Emergency. If someone is suddenly and unexpectedly placed in danger and does not have time to consider all the facts and circumstances, he will not be held to the same standard of care as if the emergency did not exist, and had he had time to weigh the available options.

Evidence. Testimony and exhibits at trial which relate to the transactions sued upon, offered by a party to prove his or her points.

Expert. A witness who, through experience, education, training, or any combination of them, has knowledge of a particular subject beyond that of normal people.

Fair Market Value. The price an item will bring at a sale when the seller is not required to sell, and the buyer is free not to buy.

False Imprisonment. Unlawful detention of a person for any length of time; a wrongful loss of personal liberty.

Gambling. A contract which induces people to risk their money or property on chance. Since the contract is null and void, the loser usually has the right to recover his losses by filing a civil action. Varies from state to state.

Gift. To be a valid gift, the giver must intend to give the thing without condition, the receiver must accept it, and there must be some kind of delivery. An engagement ring is usually a gift, although the argument has been successfully made in some states that the gift is conditioned on completion of the marriage. If it is still on layaway at the store, there has been no delivery, therefore, no gift.

Hearsay. A statement made by a witness in court that states what someone else said outside of court; the value of the statement has nothing to do with the witness's credibility in the courtroom. Hearsay can become part of the evidence in a case only under limited legal circumstances or because of necessity. (Therefore, argue that it's necessary if you must use it.)

Implied Contract. An agreement inferred from the actions of the parties, as a matter of reason and justice. If the parties act like they have a contract, and one party relies on that and is harmed, justice may demand that he be treated as if the contract had been actually agreed to.

Impossibility. When one party to a contract's promise is to perform some act or series of acts, and that act has become impossible, he or she will be excused. (Note: *Impossible* here means impossible, not merely impractical.) If the other party parted with something of value in reliance on the promised performance, he or she will be have the value restored inasmuch as it can be.

Intentional Infliction of Emotional Distress. Known as *outrage* in some states. the wrongdoer intentionally inflicts provable psychological damage on the victim.

Interference with a Business. A right to recover exists for the malicious, wrongful interference with a business. Differs from mere competition because of the malice involved.

Joint Liability. When two or more persons act jointly with resulting harm, each can be held liable for the whole resulting damage. If two or more people sign a contract, say a lease, with a third party, say a landlord, the landlord can recover the full loss of rent from any of them.

Libel. See *Defamation*.

Lien. A right granted by a statute to hold property as security for a debt and sell it if the debt is not satisfied.

Lost Property. Mislaid property that is involuntarily separated from an owner who does not know where it is. The finder is required to try to locate the owner and return it before it is considered *lost*, and the finder may claim it.

Malicious Prosecution. A tort committed by beginning and prosecuting a criminal action against another without factual basis.

Mediation. A procedure to effect settlement where the parties meet with a person disinterested in the case, the mediator, who assists them in reaching a settlement. Mandatory in some courts.

Misrepresentation of Facts. Not actionable unless the facts are worthy of belief. Not actionable if the facts are about future events, since no one can predict the future. Is fraud if there is proof that the promisor, at the time the promise to perform in the future is made, had no present intention to perform later.

Negligence. The countless situations where people's carelessness causes damage.

Notice. A successfully communicated fact.

Nuisance. An annoyance producing object or activity.

Partnership. A contract between at least two people or businesses to pool their assets and share profits and losses in some enterprise.

Principal. An *Agent's* employer. For example, if a hardware store clerk accidently drops a 16-oz. hammer on your toe while explaining its merit to you, the hardware store owner is the principal, and he or she can be held liable for your injury.

Proof. Any matter that tends to sway the mind toward believing the truth or falsity of another fact or proposition.

Repossession. A creditor's right to seize property that has been pledged as security for a debt. If a creditor seizes property but does not have a clear right to, he does it at his risk and may be liable for wrongful interference of the debtor's property. Rule: Always be careful before you take the law into your own hands.

Security Interest. The property right given when someone pledges property as security for a debt or other obligation. If you get one, you become a *secured party*. See *Collateral*.

Self Defense. A person is justified in using such reasonable force as is necessary to repel or prevent bodily harm at the hands of another.

Subcontractor. A worker who contracts to do a specific job for a general contractor. The general contractor has the contract with the property or business owner to do the whole job.

Statute of Frauds. A state statute that requires certain matters to be in writing so as to prevent fraud. Applies to deeds, promises to pay other's debts, some leases, real estate sales contracts, and the like.

Slander. See Defamation.

Statute of Limitations. A number of years set by statute beyond which the right to file a law suit for a legal claim expires. For example, actions on simple written contracts, six years; oral contracts, four years; personal injuries, two years; claims against doctors, one year. Vary from state to state.

Stop Payment. Before a bank pays it, the person who writes a check can order the bank not to pay it. The bank must honor this request of its customer. The stop payment does not change the obligation the check was written for in the first place.

Tort. A wrongful act resulting in injury to another's person, property, or reputation for which the injured party is entitled to seek compensation. See Chapter 7.

Voir Dire. The examination of a proposed witness or juror to ascertain the person's competence to give or hear testimony.

Waiver. Voluntarily giving up a known right, such as a right to sue. Once given up, it cannot be reclaimed.

Appendix 3

STATE COURTS AND QUIRKS

State	Courts and Quirks	Jurisdiction Amount
Alabama	District Courts. Seats in each county and in each city having population of 1,000 or more where no District Court sits. Up to $10,000; if less than $3,000, must be brought here The general rules of civil procedure apply. No juries. Appeal to Circuit Court within 14 days of judgment. New trial on appeal. A bond is required in twice the amount for appeal. Filing fee: $50.	$3,000/$10,000
Alaska	Magistrate Courts sit in each of four judicial district with small claims courts in specified towns. Usual civil procedure applies. No formal pleadings. Parties required to be advised that mediation, conciliation and arbitration services available. Filing fee: $15.	$5,000

Arizona	Justice Courts. Counties are divided into justice precincts, each with a Justice of the Peace. General rules of civil procedure apply. There is a small claims division within each Justice Court where trials are had before a hearing officer without attorneys. Filing Fee: $11. Service Fee: $11. Trial within 60 days of Answer. The result is final and binding. Municipal courts have same jurisdiction as Justice Courts where the city or town encompasses the entire precinct. No attorneys unless the parties agree.	$5,000 $1,500 $5,000
Arkansas	Common Pleas Courts are established in certain counties by special legislation. County and probate judges hear the cases. Civil Justice Courts in counties and townships: Must be filed here if for under $100; p to $300. May order property returned; personal property damage limit $100; Municipal Courts may be established in cities of 2,400 or more or in county seats of less than 2,400 by ordinance. Can hear same cases as in Civil Justice Courts and other cases up to $3,000. Municipal judges or city magistrates hear cases in their "small claims division." Judgment may include an order for the delivery of property. Collection agencies and assignees can't sue here. Police Courts in other cities of 2nd class. Forms provided by clerk.	$1,000 $300/$100 $3,000
California	Municipal and Justice Courts. Each county establishes its own districts. Except in San Diego, no city has more than one district. Some counties have both municipal and Justice courts. Mandatory arbitration. Full trial available after arbitration. Small claims court: Municipal court judges and justice court judges hear cases, where there is no municipal court. Money damages only. A party may not	$25,000 $5,000

California *continued*	file more than two claims for more than $2,500 in any calendar year. Court may cancel contract, award restitution, or order contract performed. Assignees of claims may not sue here. No attorneys or persons other than a party may file. Advisers available to litigants upon request at no charge. Full new trial available to superior court, but no appeal is available from that decision.	
Colorado	County courts. No boundary disputes or other cases involving title to realty. Notice of Appeal to district court must be filed 15 days after judgment. Filing fee $26, docket fee for defendant, $31. Fees go up with value of case. Small Claims Division of County Court in every county. No attorneys unless a party or agent of a corporation. No defamation, slander. Unless objected to, cases tried by referees/attorneys appointed for this purpose. Informal rules. Plaintiff limited to two actions a month or 18 per year. Mediation services available.	10,000 $5,000
Connecticut	Small Claims Division of Superior Court. Heard by magistrates. Informal pleadings. Transfers available to other courts for jury trial. May by agreement submit claim to a commissioner for speedy hearing. Commissioner not bound by rules of evidence.	$2,000
Delaware	Justice of the Peace courts in each county. Court of common pleas. No jury trials available in either court.	$15,000 $50,000
District of Columbia	Small Claims and Conciliation Division of Superior Court. Must file here if under $2,000.	$2,000
Florida	Small Claims Division of County Courts handle small claims.	$5,000

Georgia	Magistrate Courts in each County. Lawyers can appear. Informal pleadings, Rules of Civil Procedure do not apply. Filing Fee $25, plus service. Installment payments on judgments available.	$5,000
Hawaii	District Courts in each of four districts. No jury. Appeal to Superior Court or intermediate appeals court. Small Claims Division includes landlord/tenant, actions for repair, to reform or rescind contracts. Counterclaims up to $20,000 allowed. Jury trial demand requires transfer to Circuit Court. With permission, any person may appear on behalf of another. Judge not bound by rules of evidence except as it relates to privileged communications. Service by certified mail.	$10,000 $2,500
Idaho	Small Claims Department in Magistrate Division of the seven District Courts. Filing fee $18. Appeal within 30 days to another lawyer magistrate different from one who rendered judgment. Winner entitled to $25 attorney fee.	$3,000
Illinois	Small Claims in any of 21 Circuit Courts. When for less than $1,000, a party may move for informal resolution by court without rules of procedure or evidence. Service by certified mail. Appearance of Defendant on trial date is all that is necessary, but Answers can be filed. Jury of 6 or 12 available. Discovery only with court permission. Judgments may be paid in installments for up to three years.	$2,500
Indiana	Small Claims and Misdemeanor Division of Superior Court in each county. Landlord/tenant. Informal trials. Informal procedure and evidence except for privileged communications.	$3,000

Iowa	District Associate Judges of eight judicial districts hear cases, use judicial magistrate rules of procedure. "Small claim" is action for up to $4,000. Defendant must appear 20 days after filing. Installment payment judgments and appeal available.	$5,000 $4,000
Kansas	District Courts in each county. Magistrate hears. New trial on appeal to District Court judges. Small Claims Procedure Act applies. $19.50 filing fee for claims of $500 or less; $39.50 for $500-$1,000. No lawyers. Only 10 claims/person/year allowed. Loser must provide clerk with list of assets and debts within 30 days. Appeal to District Court within 30 days for new trial.	$10,000 $1,800
Kentucky	Small Claims Division in each of 56 districts. No libel or slander, alienation of affections, malicious prosecution. Collection agents and commercial lenders not allowed. Attorneys okay. No formal pleadings or discovery. No jury. Informal appeal to Circuit Court in the district.	$1,500
Louisiana	Parish Courts and City Courts have $10,000 limit; Ville Platte and Lafayette, $5,000. City Courts can evict, order rent payments up to $500 per week. Informal pleadings in City and Parish Courts when claim is $2,000 or less. Justice of the Peace Courts have $2,000 limit. Informal pleadings. Answer in 10 days. Jury demand transfers case to District Court. Appeal from Parish J.P., Small Claims, and City Courts to Parish Court for new trial; if none to District Court. 39 District Courts have concurrent jurisdiction with these others up to $5,000. No discovery.	$10,000 $2,000 $5,000

Maine	Small Claims Courts in each of 13 districts. Technical rules of evidence do not apply; rules of procedure do. Payments of judgments in installments of not less than $15 available.	$3,000
Maryland	Small Claims Courts in each of 12 districts. One judge in each county. $10 filing fee for claims of $500 or less; $15 for more than $500. Jury available if over $500. Landlord suits for rent less than $2,500. Appeal to Circuit Court in County or Baltimore City for new trial in 30 days.	$2,500
Massachusetts	Small Claims Division of District Courts in each county. Filing fee $10 if for less than $500; $15 if more. File here if claim is less than $2,000, though double or triple damages may be had in counterclaim. No jury trials. May be removed to regular civil court on request. Plaintiff who files here waives right to jury trial and to appeal to jury. Loser may file jury demand within 10 days for jury of six: requires $100 surety bond be posted. May order payments in installments. Uniform Small Claims Rules apply.	$2,000
Michigan	Small Claims Division of District Court in each county. District judges hear cases. Substantial justice applied. No libel, fraud, slander, intentional torts. No attorneys except who represent themselves. No collection agencies. No right to jury trial or appeal. Either party may demand removal to district court regular docket to retain these rights. Accepting small claims procedure waives rights to counsel, jury, appeal.	$1,750
Minnesota	Conciliation Court of Civil Division of County Court. Informal procedure. Attorneys allowed, not customary. Appeal to Court of Appeals. Municipal Courts in Hennepin, Ramsey Counties offer alternative dispute resolution.	$7,500

Mississippi	Justice Courts holds court at least once a month. Practice and procedure same as in Circuit Courts.	$2,500
Missouri	In each county, Associate Circuit Court Judge has small claims docket. Attorneys not necessary. Short informal hearing. Cases can be heard by agreement with no document filing. For any claim above $3,000, plaintiff may file as a small claim, but waives higher claim amount in later hearings. If counterclaim exceeds $3,000, with consent of both, judge can hear it all. No assignee parties. Max 8 claims per year. $10 filing fee, $5 if for less than $100. Service by certified mail. No answer necessary if defendant appears on date shown on summons. If found that suit was brought for harassment, party can be barred from filing further claims for up to a year. Appeal to Circuit Court. Court of the city of St. Louis is a separate circuit.	$3,000
Montana	At least one Justice of the Peace court in each county. Montana Justice and City Court Rules apply. City Courts in cities of over 4,000 people. Answer in 20 days. Max 10 claims per year. Pamphlets explaining procedure attached to copy of complaint for plaintiff, served on defendant. Appeal to Justice Court. Small claims court. No lawyers. Defendant may remove to Justice of the Peace Court within 10 days of service. Failure to remove waives right to counsel and jury. Appeal to District Court.	$5,000 $3,000
Nebraska	County Courts. County and City Courts have small claims departments. No attorneys. No assignee parties. If counterclaim is for more than $1500, whole case transferred to County Court. No formal pleadings or rules of evidence except for privileged communications. Fee $9, plus service.	$15,000 $2,100

State	Description	Amount
Nevada	Justice Courts in townships. Rules of Civil Procedure apply. City Courts may be established in incorporated cities or towns. Up to $5,000 if case is for mechanic's lien. Justice Court Rules of Procedure apply. Small Claims Court in each Justice Court. No attorneys except in civil shoplifting cases.	$7,500 $5,000 $3,500
New Hampshire	Each county divided into districts, with small claims court in each. Jury trial available for claims over $1,500 . No technical rules of evidence. Judgments payable in installments.	$2,500
New Jersey	Small Claims Section, Special Civil Part, Law Division, Superior Court in each County. Appeals to Small Claims Section, Appellate Division, Superior Court. Any city or two or more may establish Municipal Courts. Contract matters not exceeding $100.	$2,000 $100
New Mexico	Counties of more than 200,000 have Metropolitan Courts. Jury available. Appeal to District Court within 30 days of judgment. Magistrate Courts in all counties of less than 200,000. Jury of 6 available. Appeal within 15 days to District Court for New Trial. Magistrate Court rules apply. Bond required if appeal is filed.	$5,000 $2,000
New York	Justice Courts in most towns. Small Claims Courts in each borough of New York City, each district of Nassau County and Suffolk County, except the 1st. No assignees or insurers. Corporations only if Defendants. Filing fee $10 for claims less than $1,000; $15 if for more. Service by certified mail. Max 5 actions per year. Judgments payable into court to be disbursed in installments. Commercial Claims Parts handle corporate, association, or partnership claims. Filing fee $3, plus mailing cost. Jury available on demand.	$3,000 $2,000

North Carolina	Magistrate Courts in each of 30 Districts. For recovery of money or personal property, eviction. Appeal to District Court for New Trial.	$3,000
North Dakota	County Courts in each county seat. Each has Board of Conciliation to aid in settlement. No power to require it. Small Claims Division of County Courts, for recovery of money, cancellation of agreements from fraud.	$10,000 $2,000
Ohio	Court of Common Pleas in each county. Subject to transfer to City Court if claims less than $1,000. City Courts and County Courts in all counties where city does not cover whole county. Must file here if for less than $500. Small Claims Courts in each City and County Court. Referee may reside. Lawyers okay. Counterclaims up to $1,500. Payment of judgments in installments on request. Filing fees vary. No juries.	$10,000 $3,000 $1,000
Oklahoma	Small Claims Division in each of 26 District Courts. No collection agencies or assignees. Small Claims Procedure Act applies. Defendant may transfer to regular docket for $50 fee. If Defendant transfers and Plaintiff wins, Plaintiff gets attorney's fees. Filing fees vary. Defendant pays $5 for counterclaim or claim of set off.	$4,500
Oregon	Each justice and District Court has Small Claims Division. Must be in small claims if for less than $200. Up to $2,500 may be heard here or in District Court. District Court claims require affidavit that plaintiff made a bona fide effort to collect before filing. Answer in 14 days. If Defendant doesn't answer, Plaintiff awarded extra $50 as prevailing party fee. Jury request by Defendant causes dismissal, Plaintiff has 20 days to file in District Court. No lawyers without court consent.	$10,000 $2,500

Pennsylvania	District Justices in all 60 districts but Philadelphia County (where municipal court sits); a district judge in each magisterial district. Philadelphia Municipal Court. Community Courts: Electors in any district may establish court with judge power the same as District Court.	$4,000 $10,000 $4,000
Puerto Rico	Court of First Instance in each of 13 judicial regions. Governor appoints 90-126 judges for civil cases in superior and Municipal Courts. Summary procedure available under Rule 60.	$2,000
Rhode Island	District Court. Must be filed here if less than $5,000; here or in Superior Court if up to $10,000. Appeal to Superior Court must be filed in 2 days. Service by certified mail. No jury. Small claims for damages from retail sales, or upon negotiable instruments. Filing fee: $5, plus postage.	$10,000 $1,500
South Carolina	Magistrate Courts. Magistrate Court rules apply. Answer in 30 days, 5 days of claim is for $25 or less. Jury of 6 available. Appeal to Circuit Court within 30 days.	$5,000
South Dakota	Small claims procedure available in each of 8 Circuit Courts, and Magistrate Courts. Fees $4, $10, and $20 for claims up to $100, $1,000, and over $1,000 respectively. Attorneys permitted. No jury in Magistrate Court. Judgments payable in installments.	$4,000
Tennessee	Courts of General Session $10,000 limit; $15,000 in counties of at least 700,000. Trial Justice Courts in Anderson, Dyer, Gibson, and Montgomery Counties.	$10,000 $15,000 varies

State	Description	Amount	
Texas	From 2-8 Justice Courts in each County. May order return of property. Each Justice of the Peace has a small claims court. Forms provided. Commercial lenders and collection agencies may not sue. Appeal is to a new trial.	$5,000	
Utah	Small Claims are departments of 8 District and County Justice Courts. Filing fee: $15, plus service fee based on mileage. Filing fees $37 for claims of $2,000 or less, $80 for $2,000-10,000. Defendant appears between 5-45 days; trial 10-20 days after Answer. Appeal to District Court within 10 days for new trial. Small claims procedural rules also govern appeals.	$10,000	$2,000
Vermont	Small Claims Courts part of District Courts in each county. Filing fee $35 if for more than $500; $25, if less. Jury available when requested by Defendant for $10. Must file here if claim is for $1,000 or less.	$3,500	
Virgin Islands	Small Claims Division of at least one Territorial Court per island. Must be filed here if for less than $500. Informal procedure.	$5,000	
Virginia	General District Courts in 31 districts. Procedure follows Supreme Court Rule 3D. Small Claims Courts in any district meeting certain population requirements or created by ordinance.	$10,000	$1,000
Washington	At least one District Court in each county. Municipal Courts in each city of 400,000. Every District Court has small claims department. $10 filing fee. Lawyers forbidden. Informal hearings. No appeal if amount is less than $100, nor by losing plaintiff if less than $1,000.	$25,000 $25,000 $2,500	

West Virginia	County Magistrate Courts in each county. Not for false imprisonment, malicious prosecution, libel or slander. Accepts credit cards for court costs.	$5,000
Wisconsin	No small claims courts. Small claims procedure available in civil cases and evictions, actions for the return of property and for earnest money. Jury of 6 available when filing answer for extra fee; must be demanded within 20 days of filing answer. Fees include 45 justice information system fee, $2 special court clerks fee and $40 court support services fee. Appeal to Court of Appeal.	$5,000
Wyoming	Justices' Courts in each county. Special jurisdiction here if for not more than $2,000. $4 filing fee. Defendant must appear between 3-12 days from service. Informal hearing. Appeal to District Court. County Courts in the 12 counties of more than 30,000 people replace justice courts.	$3,000 $2,000 $7,000

Information and selection and organization of information originally appeared in the United States Law Digest® section of the MARTINDALE-HUBBELL Law Directory, © Reed Elsevier Inc., and is used with permission of Reed Reference Publishing, a division of Reed Elsevier, Inc.

Index

A

Accident, 163
Action number, 29
Affidavit, 163
   for entry of default judgment, 146
Agent for service, 99
Allegations, 28
Alternate Dispute Resolution, 90
Answer and counterclaim, 145, 149,
Answer, 28
   filing, 103
   filing time, 100
   possible responses, 101-103
Arbitration, 90
Arbitrator, 26
Assault and battery, 44
Attorney
   friend, 23
   hiring an, 91-94
   novice, 23
   pettifogger, 22
   small claims, 92

B

Bailiff, 29, 105-106
Bailment, contract of, 68
Bankruptcy, 35
   collecting your claim and, 140-141
Best evidence rule, the, 116
Breach of contract, 163
Burden of proof, 163
Business docket, 139
Business forms, 98-99

C

Case number, 29
Cause of action, 28, 33-38, 43
Character evidence, 163
Choosing a jury, 124-126, 133-134
Civil wrongs, 40-41
Claims
   personal injury, 44
   types of, 39-41
Clerk of court, 29
Clerk, questions to ask, 161-162
Closing statement, 125, 133

Collateral, 163

Commercial docket, 139

Complaint, 25, 28, 69, 97, 99, 100, 145, 147

Consent agreement, 101

Consent judgment, 146, 155

Consent judgment payment agreement, 156

Consent order, 146, 152
dismissal after, 146, 153

Constable, 29 (see also *Deputy Sheriff*)

Constitutional rights, 35

Contentions, 28 (see also *Allegations*)

Contract and tort combinations, 67-70

Contract cases, 57-65

Contract, 28, 47-55, 164
implied, 165
oral, 49

Contributory negligence, 164

Conversion, tort of, 68

Corporation, 37, 164

Counterclaim, 28, 102

Court clerk, 75, 76, 105

Court, power of, 98

Courthouse, the, 105-106

Courtroom clerk, 105

Cross-examination, 120-124, 130

D

Defamation, 164

Default judgment, affidavit for entry of, 146, 154

Default, 28
affidavit and notice of, 146, 158

Defendant, 25, 28

Demand letters, 79

Deputy sheriff, 29

Discovery, 26, 103-104, 164
post-judgment, 138

E

Emotional distress, 165

Evidence, 164

Exemplary damages, 69
(see also *Punitive damages*)

Exhibits, 115-118,
admission into evidence, 129

Expert testimony, 93

Expert witnesses, 113-114, 119, 164
questions to ask, 114-115

F

Facts, 40

Failure to respond, 103

Fair market value, 37, 164

Fairness, 40

File, 29

File number, 29

Franklin, Ben, 13

Fraud, 28

Fraud and deceit, cases of, 68
proving, 92-93

G

Garnishment, 140

General execution docket, 139

Getting to Yes, 90

Gift, 37

H

Hearsay, 112, 117, 118, 165
business records as, 119
certified court documents as, 119

Human factor in a trial, the, 83

I

Implied contract, 165
Interrogatories, 138-139
  refusal to answer, 139

J

Joint liability, 165
Judges, 29, 40, 82
Judgment, 29, 80, 84
  collection of, 84, 102, 137-141
  collection and bankruptcy, 140-141
  collectibility of, 72
Judgment by default, 103
Judgment creditor, 137
Judgment debtor, 137
Judgment lien, 137
Judgment payment agreement, 146, 157
Jurisdiction, 27
  broad, 27
  general, 27

L

Law and Order, 21
Law suits, frivolous, 34
Lawyer referral services, 77, 94
Lawyers, corrupt, 91
Lawyers, hiring of, 91-94
Legal advice, 75-78
Legal claim, 28 (see also *Cause of action*)
Legal information, sources of, 76-78
"Lemon Law," 52
Levy, 139
Liability, joint, 165
Libel, 46

Lien, 64, 82, 165
  materialman's, 82
  possessory, 82
Limited liability partnership, 99
Limited partnership, 99
Liquidated damages, 103
Long Arm Statute, 98
Losing, 125

M

Magistrate, 29 (see also *Judge*)
Magnuson-Moss Warranty Act, 52
Malicious prosecution, 165
Marshall, 29 (see also *Deputy sheriff*)
Mediation, 90, 166
Mediator, 26
Mini-trial, 26, 90
Misrepresentation of facts, 166
Motion, 28

N

Negligence, 28, 166
Negotiating a settlement, 87-90
  haggling, 87-88
  interest-based, 87, 88-89
  making counteroffers, 88
Notice, 166
Nuisance, 166

O

Objections, 118-120, 129
Opening statement, 111
Opinion, 40
Opinion vs. fact, 40
Order, 28, 101

P

"Paper Sack Rule," 50, 59

Parties, 28

Payment agreement, 146

Perry Mason, 21

Personal injury claims, 44

Petition for relief, 28 (see also *Complaint*)

Plaintiff, 25, 101-103

   is right, 101-102

   third party, 148

Post-judgment discovery, 138

Private wrongs, 40-41

Procedural law, 28

Process server, 28

Professional association, 99

Proof, 166

Punitive damages, 69, 93

Q

Questions to ask the clerk, 100, 161-162

R

Reasonable doubt, 72

Rebuttal evidence, 123, 130

Redirect examination, 113

Referral services, 77, 94

Restitution, 71-72

S

Security interest, 166

Self-defense, 166

Settlement, 79-85

   negotiation tactics, 87-90

Settlement discussions, admissability of, 119

Slander, 46

Small claims courts, 25

Small claims suit, filing, 97-104

Statement of claim, 28 (see also *Complaint*)

Statute of frauds, 50, 166

Statute of limitations, 166

Statutes, criminal, 71

Subcontractor, 166

Subpoenas, 29, 100-101

Substantive Law, 28-29

Sued, being, 101

Suing a corporation, 99

Suing a partnership, 98

Suing the individual, 98

Summons, 28, 100, 145, 148

T

Third party complaint, 103, 145, 150

Third party defendant, 145

Third party plaintiff, 145

Tort and contract combinations, 67-70

Tort, 28, 43-46, 167

   attractive nuisances, 45

   nuisances, 45

   proving, 43

   trespass, 45

Tort of conversion, 68

Trial notebook, 127-134

Trial, 29

    preparation for, 109-126

U

U.S. Supreme Court, 27

Uniform Commercial Code
    (UCC) docket, 139

Uniform Commercial Code
    Financing Statement, 139

Unliquidated damages, 46, 103

V

Voir dire, 124, 167

W

Waiver, 167

Warranties, 52

    on repairs, 37

    on used goods, 36

White collar crimes, 71

Winning, 125-126

Witness statments,
    handling inconsistent, 123

Witnesses, 112-115

    badgering the, 120

NOTES

NOTES

NOTES

NOTES

MP248-TN